I UNDERSTAND WHY YOU WOULD WANT ME BUT WHY WOULD I WANT YOU?

The women's guide to working through failed relationships to reclaiming her identity.

Tiffany Marie Smith

I Understand Why You Would Want Me But Why Would I Want You? Copyright 2021 by Tiffany Smith. All rights reserved. No part of this publication may be reproduced, distributed, or transmitted in any form or by any means, including photocopying, recording, or other electronic or mechanical methods, without the prior written permission of the publisher, except in the case of brief quotations embodied in critical reviews and certain other noncommercial uses permitted by copyright law.

For permission requests, write to the publisher, addressed "Attention: Permissions Coordinator," 205 N. Michigan Avenue, Suite #810, Chicago, IL 60601. 13th & Joan books may be purchased for educational, business or sales promotional use. For information, please email the Sales Department at sales@13thandjoan.com.

Printed in the U. S. A.

First Printing, xx.

Library of Congress Cataloging-in-Publication Data has been applied for.

ISBN: 978-1-953156-30-3

Contents

CHAPTER 1
Every Heartbreak Begins with Love 5

CHAPTER 2
Intention Setting and Manifestation After A Divorce/Breakup 21

CHAPTER 3
The Journey of Being Numb 27

CHAPTER 4
Start A New Life 41

CHAPTER 5
A Breakup to Queen Up Story Queen Sasha's Story 59

CHAPTER 6
Why Are Breakups So Painful? 73

CHAPTER 7
Queen Sasha's Breakthrough 87

CHAPTER 8
No Baby Mama Drama Over Here 99

CHAPTER 9
A Breakup to Queen Up Story Queen Michelle's Story 119

CHAPTER 10
How to Deal with the Pain of a Breakup 129

CHAPTER 11
Queen Michelle's Lesson 143

CHAPTER 12
The Rainbow at the End of the Storm 155

Prologue

Dear Queen,
   When I sit and think about my past I see so many errors that I made. I also see so many lessons that I needed to learn to help me with my healing. Yes, I'm the female that believes that after a divorce, a breakup, the ending of a situationship, time to heal is needed. However, it took me almost two years to realize how important my healing process was. When I first got out of my marriage, my first response was, "Okay, let the casual dating begin!"

   In hindsight, that may not have been the best first step. I began dating prematurely. And what premature dating really means is I brought my broken, unhealed baggage to the table and tried to be the person I was before I got hurt. I was very foolish to believe that I could just jump back into my dating life.. and it showed!

   Truthfully, my dating experience wasn't 100 percent horrible before I healed, but I started to realize that I was moving in a way that wasn't really me. Luckily, some people were more patient than others because I am a "catch"... I was just an "unhealed catch."

   My divorce led me to the journey of getting to know a version of myself… the best version. Getting to know what I like and don't like. Trying out new adventures, doing things I always wanted to do but was too afraid.

I UNDERSTAND WHY

And that's what I want for you.

This book is for every female that has gotten her heart broken at the hands of love.

Love is a four-letter word that we as females have been conditioned to search for and to feel less than if we never have it or had it and lost it.

I want to assist you with resetting your mind from the thought that love has to come from an outside source to you must first love yourself from within.

Let me tell you a little about my story

I was married, and it was hard. I wasn't happy, and I don't think he was happy either. During my marriage I struggled with feeling ungrateful! Why was I feeling ungrateful? Because there are a lot of women out there that want someone of their own, want to be a bride, want a husband, and I had that... but I wasn't happy. I felt very ungrateful. I was raised with both parents who have been married for 30 something years and are still going strong. I had to learn that ending a relationship doesn't mean you are a failure or ungrateful. It means that you are wise enough to assess the situation and remove yourself from it because you know you and your partner both deserve true happiness.

During this book it might feel a little like story time as I share stories about my life, stories that were shared with me, and different lessons that were learned along the way. Through various stories and lessons learned, this book will make you laugh, relate, and reflect on your journey to becoming the queen you are meant to be.

From Break Up to Queen Up

I used to know the girl whose smile touched her eyes
I used to know the woman who held her head up with pride
I used to know the lady whose walk could silence the crowd
They were all me
We were like the trinity; one of the same
But through heartbreaks we became broken
My soul knew broken was never to remain
Through long nights of precious tears fallen
I water myself
I grow into the Queen that I was destined to become
I take my throne with no guilt, shame, or regrets.
For I know that L doesn't stand for losses but for lessons learned
You see, Lessons are the stepping stones that lead to the throne
Grateful I am
Humble I will always be
But never mistake the powerfulness of a Queen who regained her identity

1

Every Heartbreak Begins with Love

*"Father God, I'm not sure what I'm supposed to be doing
at this point. I'm not happy, my marriage is falling apart.
I need your help."*
"Tiffany, Leave Him"

Pause.... Let's rewind so you can understand how I got to this point in my life.

Hey—My name is Tiffany, and I am divorced.

Whew, that was easy!

Naw, but seriously my name is Tiffany, and I am a breakup coach—but more importantly, I am a coach who assists women with regaining their identity.

Now you may ask *What does that mean?* And here is your answer. I assist women on various journeys of life to find themselves.

Have you ever felt that you have strayed away from the person you were meant to be? Have you ever felt that you have a purpose, but somewhere along the way you fell off track? If you are like most women at some time in their life, then yes, you have felt this way. And if you haven't, good for you! But don't close this book just yet; you may also learn something about your journey through my many lessons.

I UNDERSTAND WHY

Now back to my prayer.

I got married at the age of 28. My ex-husband and I were friends since freshman year of high school. Technically I knew him since elementary school, but it wasn't until our 9th grade year that we became super close. Let's give the ex the name Best Friend. Back in high school Best Friend and I would talk on the phone every day. We never really hung out because my parents didn't play that boyfriend while in high school game, and we didn't even live in the same area as one another. Somehow our long talks on the phone every night until my mom would pick up the landline and say her famous line, "Tiffany, your time is up," blossomed into two teenagers that really cared for one another.

We were young, but I knew Best Friend and my friendship was special. I was able to talk to him about anything. No matter how silly or vain, he always listened.

During our high school years we attempted dating, but it didn't work out. We stayed friends nonetheless and continued to speak on the phone every single night. The only time I can recall Best Friend and I not talking on the phone was when he would get upset for whatever reason and disappear for weeks/months at a time. I never understood why Best Friend would disappear, but I always called him daily and would get denied access. Somehow, no matter how long Best Friend stayed away, I always had open arms and allowed him back in my life whenever he saw fit to come back.

As a teenager, I had no clue to the cycle I was allowing and definitely never questioned myself on why I would allow someone to enter and exit my life as they pleased. But this was actually an issue I had throughout the majority of my life, with relationships and friendships. I constantly allowed people to leave and come back with open arms, not holding them accountable for carelessly hurting my feelings and not holding myself accountable for not knowing my worth.

Best Friend was a repeat offender even once we started dating in our twenties. I could never understand why he would break up with me for no reason. But each time he would leave me crushed. It hurt like hell. And each time I thought the answer to my broken heart was dating a new person. I don't think I ever gave my heart time to heal from any of my previous relationships either. Back then I called it me being a "relationship girl"—you know, the type of female that likes to be with one person and not dating around or having time to herself. It sounded good at the time. But in all reality I was just adding more bad habits that I would eventually have to work through.

I'll never forget Best Friend's last disappearing act. We were four years into our on-again, off-again dating relationship. It was on June 29th, exactly one day before my birthday. For two whole weeks I had to deal with a distant boyfriend for reasons unknown. I would text, and he would respond with one or two words. I would call, but he wouldn't be interested in the conversation. So finally I sent a text addressing his lack of interest.

> Me: Hey... so I'm not sure what's going on but you aren't being your normal self
> Best Friend: I have a lot on my mind
> Me: Like what?
> Best Friend: Stuff
> Me: What's going on?? What aren't you telling me?
> Best Friend:...
> Me: Do you not want to be with me anymore?
> Best Friend: ....

I UNDERSTAND WHY

Me: Hello?!!!
Best Friend: I didn't want to do this before your birthday.
Best Friend: I think we should breakup
Me: Ok

Before I sent the okay text, I texted a friend saying that he broke up with me. Within the next 20 minutes I was set up for a blind birthday date for the next day.

I don't think I cried right away, but my birthday morning I was crushed. I was in disbelief that this man that I loved, had known for over a decade of my life and dated for over four years, who was supposed to be my best friend, broke up with me the day before my birthday.

But in typical Tiffany fashion, I dated other people and attempted to move on.

Four months later I received a message on Facebook messenger.

Best Friend: Hey

I was psyched! My Best Friend hit me up, and I was so happy that he was back.

By June 30th of the following year I was engaged and ready to be Mrs. Best Friend.

I thought this was the best decision ever. I loved him and he loved me. We were best friends… Isn't this what fairy tales look like?

Before we got married, Best Friend and I completed premarital counseling. Our sessions with the counselor went smoothly up until she asked about any issues we were worried about seeing in our marriage.

I answered, "Sometimes he disappears and I need him to know that he can't disappear when we are married."

Best Friend responded with a simple, "Yes, I know I can't disappear once we're married."

And all was well.

To be honest, my concern should have been, "Sometimes he disappears and I need to know why. What causes all his disappearing acts?!"

But I didn't; I was too young and naïve to understand that there was an underlying issue. An issue that was going to be the barrier of this marriage ending with "and they lived together happily ever after."

Anyways...Best Friend and I had an intimate wedding. It was only our mothers, his brother, my two sisters, and my youngest niece and nephew. The day was interesting. Best Friend and his mom had a close relationship, and I'm not sure that she was ready to fully share her son. And to add to it, I also moved into her home.

I moved my belongings into Best Friend's mother's home on our wedding day. I was ready for this journey of forever that I was sure we were going to have.

Best Friend's and my marriage started out okay. I was for sure that we were good. If we had a disagreement, we would talk about it. Yeah, it took some time, but eventually we were always able to work through whatever the issue was. As time went on, I started to notice that rebounding from disagreements weren't as easy, and Best Friend started to get frustrated with the smallest things. I couldn't make sense of it.

I worked as a social worker and prided myself on having calm, nonjudgmental conversations during trying times. During my

I UNDERSTAND WHY

marriage I practiced patience and tried to have an open mind to how and why Best Friend felt and reacted the way he did.

Our main issue was that when Best Friend became upset he retreated. I guess Best Friend kept his word and didn't disappear during our marriage in the physical sense, but his retreating was its own form of disappearance.

When Best Friend retreated, he shut down. I could try to be sweet, kind, flirtatious, loving, but it didn't matter. Once Best Friend was in that mood, there was nothing I could do to get him out of it. And I would try everything. Best Friend's mood could last weeks. Which would mean we could go weeks without talking, touching, laughing, or having any meaningful interaction all while still sleeping next to one another.

It drained me.

But times with Best Friend weren't always trying. Somehow we managed to even have a second wedding for our families and friends.

Our second wedding was supposed to be a nice time. But from the planning to the actual day it was everything but.

You know sometimes you don't realize how wrong something is when you are in it. Sometimes you may overlook someone's behaviors behind closed doors. But everything that happens in the dark always comes to the light. Best Friend's mood swings were one of the things that happened in the dark, happened behind closed doors, and were kept as a secret.

Yup, no one was aware of the mood swings until wedding day number 2. Best Friend and I had just jumped the broom and were in the limo with our bridesmaids and groomsmen. There I sat happy and beautiful. I'd just said my vows in front of all my friends and family. My dress was beautiful, my hair and makeup were slayed, but that joy was short-lived. As I sat in that limo happy, living a moment I never thought would happen, there was Best Friend sitting next to me with his headphones in his ear. At first I was taken aback because I didn't understand why he had them in. So I smiled at him and he just kept listening to his music, nodding his head to the beat. I didn't understand what was going on, so I laughed and tried talking to him.

> Me: Best Friend, take off your headphones!
> Best Friend: (silent and points to his headphones as if he couldn't hear me)

I then realized that this was a mood. A mood that was geared toward me. But why? I didn't do anything. We just said our vows, and everything had gone as planned. What happened and why is he acting like this today? Why is he doing this in front of the photographer, my friends, my sisters, his boys, and his brother? His brother must have picked up on the mood because he attempted to help me out of my embarrassing moment as everyone in the limo was looking at us, unsure of what the hell was going on. My heart sank. Why couldn't he allow today to be a good day without an issue?

My high of happiness was quickly taken away as I sat in that limo in that white gown on the brink of tears. Tears because I knew this wasn't okay. Tears because the secret I'd kept from my friends and family was being exposed.

The entire limo drive, Best Friend jammed to the music blasting from his Beats by Dre headphones.

When we reached the park to take our wedding pictures, Best Friend hung out with his boys, and I kept close to my girls. We

I UNDERSTAND WHY

did good fronting for the cameras. We smiled when we were supposed to. We kissed when instructed to. We looked at each other with love in our eyes as told. But the truth of the matter is, it was all a front. Best Friend was still in a mood, and I was walking on glass trying to assess the situation.

The majority of my marriage was me walking on glass, unsure what I could say or do because I wasn't trying to upset Best Friend.

Somehow Best Friend was able to recover from his mood during the wedding reception. I think that may have been the quickest he'd ever gotten out of a funk. I later found out what caused the mood in the first place. Best Friend was upset with how one of our photographers that I hired was dressed. Best Friend ruined a memory for me because of how someone was dressed. Something I didn't have any control over.

I remember Best Friend and I would go back and forth regarding his moods. I would tell him how long he'd had a mood for, and he would deny it. I started to doubt myself.

I couldn't keep up with all the hecticness, so I began documenting his moods. I literally kept a journal of his mood swings in the back of my diary.

Moday: he looked at me but didn't speak
Tuesday: no eye contact and no words spoken

I was driving myself crazy.

An outlet I eventually had for myself was starting a business. I wanted to assist women, so I became a life coach. I started my business, Dare To B You, and even attempted to start a blog. My blog was originally called You UngratefulL Married Bish. When I put together "You Ungrateful Married Bish" I was feeling exactly what the title said... ungrateful! Why was I feeling ungrateful? Because there are a lot of women out there that want someone of their own, want to be a bride, want a husband, and I had that... but I wasn't happy. I felt very ungrateful... I was raised with both parents who have been married for 30 something years and are still going strong ... I had to learn that ending a relationship doesn't mean you are a failure or ungrateful. It means that you are wise enough to assess the situation and remove yourself from it because you know you and your partner both deserve true happiness.

As I started working on building my business, I hired a coach because I definitely didn't know what I was doing, but I was on a mission.

Unfortunately, pouring myself into my business wasn't enough to take my mind off of the issues in my marriage. Our issues grew as Best Friend's moods continued and started lasting longer and longer. I was becoming so stressed with all of our issues. During my marriage I would always suggest counseling to Best Friend, and he would always say no. But once we started talking about possibly separating, Best Friend agreed to go to counseling. First Best Friend went to counseling on his own, and I went to counseling on my own. We both were given a chance to vent and share our side of the story. Best Friend wasn't happy about going to counseling and would sometimes share that his counselor agreed with my viewpoint on the mood swings.

Eventually Best Friend and I joined our sessions and attempted working on us. Counseling wasn't helping, and our issues continued.

I eventually went to a counselling session by myself and vented about everything I was feeling still. The counselor we chose was of the Christain faith and we started and ended our sessions with a prayer. At this particular session, we were wrapping up and about to say a prayer when the counselor stopped me and said that God put something on her heart. My counselor told me that If I stayed in my marriage there would be more pain to come. A life would be lost, and if I stayed I would forever blame myself.

I was in disbelief and told her that had to be wrong because he was my best friend and we could work through this.

My counselor's response was, "Tiffany, that man is not your 'best friend.'"

I was shook.

Can you imagine being told that if you stay with the person that you'd devoted your life to it would cause pain and a loss of a loved one? And that the friendship that you had was a lie and built on bad choices?

Now I was raised in the church and went to church faithfully, but I was never that person that believes everything that someone prophesies.

I was already stressed from the many late night conversations with Best Friend begging him to reason with me, pleading for him to open up to me, and now I had to add this to my list.

What the fuck do I do?

I remember getting ready for work the next morning and one of my co-workers calling me asking me where I was at. I was supposed to be at work at 9am and it was already 10am. My behind was sitting in the basement eating cereal, checked the hell out. I was stressed. I couldn't concentrate on work, my hair was falling out, I was crying all the time, and I was gaining weight.

I eventually made it to work that day with no real reason or care for my tardiness. I was falling apart. But the worst part was that I was falling apart in complete silence. Faking happiness. Putting on a show while I felt like I was dying on the inside.

I was hurting so bad, and with the exception of two close friends, no one knew.

That Sunday came around, and I made sure I made it to church. When I got to church I just sat there.

I was all cried out.

I was numb.

I was tired of praying for my marriage to work.

The only prayer I could think to say was:

"Father God, I'm not sure what I'm supposed to be doing at this point. I'm not happy, my marriage is falling apart. I need your help."

I said my prayer to myself and just sat on the bench zoned out.

I'm not sure how much time passed, but eventually I heard Pastor Danielle say, "Tiffany, leave him."

The response caught me all the way off guard.

First of all, the church service was still going, and the pastor was preaching. And to top it off, I go to a big church and they don't know me by name, nor did they know about my marital issues.

So like any normal person I brushed it off and assumed I was so zoned out that I was hearing things.

Within the next 30 seconds of me brushing it off, I heard again: "Tiffany, leave him."

I was wide eyed at this point and if the cameras were on me I'm sure I looked like I was hearing things because I was looking around trying to figure out if anyone else in the congregation heard what the pastor had just said or if someone was playing a joke on me.

But they didn't. Everyone was tuned in to whatever the real message was.

I UNDERSTAND WHY

I couldn't fully process what was going on. I couldn't fully grasp that I was getting sign after sign to leave this man.

Even after all the signs, I tried staying with Best Friend. We weren't getting any better. I was drained. The patience and understanding ways I prided myself on having were depleted.

Best Friend and I had several disagreements throughout our relationship, but never did we really yell.

Yep, best Friend and I managed to try and stay cordial during the ending of our marriage until the last day.

It was in mid-May. Best Friend had been in a mood for three weeks, and I'd had enough. We were upstairs and I was begging and pleading with him to talk to me. I can't remember what led him to get in the mood, but he wasn't trying to communicate with me.

I sat on the floor with my back against the wall telling him how I couldn't do this anymore and I would be leaving tomorrow officially. Best Friend and I had already spoken about being separated and decided that I would continue to reside in the home because I didn't want to move back to my parents' house.

But at this point Best Friend and I couldn't live together anymore. I wanted him. I loved him. But I knew with the mood swings I wouldn't be able to stay.

Tomorrow came and I wanted to talk to Best Friend one last time. I honestly didn't want to let the marriage go. I wanted us to snap out of it and be happy again. Best Friend spoke to me briefly. Oddly enough, we talked about my birthday because it was coming up. At first I thought the conversation was going okay, then out of nowhere it went left. Best Friend and I were back to being at odds and he was leaving the house to go get a toilet seat.

I was confused. I'd asked him if the seat could wait because I was not happy, and we really needed to discuss what was going on in our relationship, but he said he had to go.

I snapped.

Best Friend was outside with his brother getting ready to hop in the car and pull off, and I went outside in a rage.

> Me: "Your wife is about to leave you and instead of taking time to talk it out you want to go get a toilet seat?"
> Best Friend: "Tiffany, the toilet seat is cracked, and it hurts to sit on. Yes I need to go get the seat now."

That man chose comfort in taking a shit over making sure I didn't leave him.

That was the last straw. I was tired of begging and pleading. I was tired of this relationship feeling one sided. I felt like I was the only one who wanted this relationship.

I packed all my belongings into my car.

Called up my parents and told them I would be coming home.

It took me two hours to pack up everything.

This man came back to the house when I was bringing down my last item.

He didn't stop me.

He helped me carry it to the car and load it in the trunk.

Once again I was too numb to feel anything.

Emotionally I was on E.

He Don't Want Me
He don't want me

I UNDERSTAND WHY

I can feel it he don't want me
It's devastating but true
He don't want me
Why can't I stop running these words through my head
It's because
He don't want me
But how is this even true
A good wife I have been
His number one cheerleader
The realist person in his life
All the others are fake and don't compare
But still
He don't want me
He don't love me
Naw that can't be true
He don't want me ...
It stings on sight
It cuts to my core
I'm burned
But not destroyed
How can I face myself in the mirror
I'm a failure
Couldn't keep the only man I loved
He's gone because he don't want me no more
He forced me to pack my shit and walk out the door
He said he didn't see the need to plead
He didn't see the purpose of saying anything worthy
I would have stayed
I'm all talk when it comes to him
One look from him and I melt

He don't get it
Why don't you see
How much you mean to me
Instead you pushed me away
Forced me to leave
Didn't want to be the bad guy
So you made me call quits
When you saw I wasn't going to fully commit
That's when you took a jab at it
My heart it breaks
My wrists are bleeding
I feel like my soul has been snatched
And this empty vessel is pleading
See I ain't too proud to beg
But I feel like I should be
I should be trying to hold on the last bit of my dignity
You did
You ain't say baby no
Baby wait
Baby don't go
Instead you weighed your options and decided
I wasn't a priority
You don't want me
But why
I felt you didn't love me so I had to say goodbye
But that shit is so hard to do
I'm dying
With a smile on my face to appease everybody
I'm drowning
Giggling but it's really me gurgling

I UNDERSTAND WHY

Death
I feel you
Sorrow
I hear you
Why don't you want me
It's a question I cannot answer
I tried
I cried
I died
No one can rescue me
I am no saint
I lied

2

Intention Setting and Manifestation After A Divorce/Breakup

Welcome to the rough side of the mountain. Even if it's your idea, breaking up is hard to do. So many emotions rise to the surface when the change involves an intimate partner. First comes the utter pain of separation; everything, positively everything changes. Unless you are the exception to the rule, even your friends are about to change. Couples make couple friends for the most part. Even the friends who choose your side will still likely be a casualty once you are single and they are not. It is the proverbial cookie crumbling.

Many of us become more open to the possibilities that The Law of Attraction and The Power of Intention can provide when we are in distress, and more so when distress is present simultaneously in several areas of our life.

It's been said that when it rains it pours, and that is exactly what happens. As soon as one area of our life falls out of balance, other areas start falling one after the other and often just as fast as a domino effect. According to The Law of Attraction and The Power of Intention, this makes total sense. Instinctively, our minds tend to focus on the problem at hand in an attempt to find a solution. This generates a "worry state" that creates negative vibrations, which in turn bring about other negative conditions in our lives.

I UNDERSTAND WHY

Are all your friends happily married and they're no help to you as you try to recover after a divorce? Did you believe your marriage would be different from others and that you and your husband would get through everything together, but now you're struggling to recover after the divorce? Do you think of him all the time and hate the thought that he may have moved on and you doubt you'll ever recover from the divorce?

Depression, mood swings, and destructive behavior is common among women who've recently divorced, and while this is particularly true of divorces brought on by the husband, it also occurs when the woman asked for the divorce. If you have no idea how to get through this and recover from the divorce, read on for a few tips that can help ease the pain and get you going in the right direction again.

RELEASING THE DREAM

As early as the first few dates, we begin to imagine and dream of the future that awaits us with our new man. Once married we continue to make plans for the future: vacations, homes, children, and even retirement. A divorce is essentially the end of those dreams as well as the end of the relationship.

Just as often as I've heard women claim to miss their ex, I've heard, "We were supposed to go to Paris next spring," "We were going to buy this beautiful house," "We'd talked about having children together." While it may be difficult to release your hold on all the dreams you had with him, you also need to realize that staying with him would not have guaranteed that those dreams come true. Let them go and prepare to build new dreams.

WORKING THROUGH THE PAIN

Though it may be tempting, the worst thing you can do at this time is to isolate yourself. A day or two of crying alone in your new apartment should not stretch out to weeks of lying around bemoaning your fate. Call up your friends, although you may want to consider opting for the friend who's been through this before.

Hearing of another woman's pain and recovery after a divorce can be enough to give you the strength you need in order to get through your own divorce. Talk it out, and let her share in your pain. Discuss those dreams you had. Sometimes the simple act of verbalizing all that we have going on in our heads is enough to diminish the weight of the pain.

DATING AGAIN

Well-intentioned friends may want to set you up in order to get you out of your funk. If you go into this with the thought of just having a fun night out, you have a better chance of having a successful date. Avoid trying to replace your husband too quickly. The majority of relationships that begin immediately after a divorce usually end in failure.

Give yourself the time to truly put your ex-husband behind you, and only face the thought of a new relationship when your mind and heart are clear of him.

Many who have gone through divorce have been displaced from their home. Rebuilding can seem an overwhelming task. Finances have been cut down, we may be moving from a house to an apartment, or even living with roommates for the first time since college days. Regardless of where we end up, though, be it a new house, moving back in with your parents, or sharing a room with a friend, we need to create a new space for ourselves to nurture our rapid new growth and thrive as a newly single person. During divorce recovery, it is especially important to attempt to create a haven where we feel protected from the demands of the world.

As we go through the task of splitting up our shared marital belongings, and the belongings find their way into the "his" and "hers" piles, the home empties in more ways than one. As we let go of a material thing, we also let go of our attachment to it. The feelings of that ugly sofa go out the door with it. The resentment of that old picture of his grandparents are packed in the box along with its chipped frame. The teapot your aunt gave you is given to Goodwill along with the guilt about never having taken it out of the box. Tossed in the dumpster are things we no longer need or want, and all the energy those things took from us.

Clearing can be very therapeutic. It leaves a space for us to recreate something better in its place. Simplifying feels good for a reason: "things" require energy. When we remove things, we often feel more peaceful because we reclaim the energy that went into owning the thing. After we release it, we give ourselves the option to either leave the space as is or fill it with something new that is useful to us in some way.

Rather than just fill the space with matching accessories, let's give thought to what it is we want from this new space.

SETTING INTENTIONS

1. **Set Intention:** First, a focused intention must be determined: without knowing what you want, it is difficult to get it. While this may seem obvious, many people have a general idea of what they want but are unable to get a clear and concrete image in their minds. At this stage, it can be helpful to write out or list your intentions. For some it is easier to create a story, draw a picture, make a song, or dance. The method does not matter as long as the intention becomes clearly defined and focused.
2. **Optimal State:** The second step in the process is to get into the optimal state—a relaxed body and a clear and focused mind are necessary to have best results. There are many techniques for achieving this, and it is important to be aware of what works for you.
3. **Make it Real:** The third step is to make the intention convincingly real, vivid, and personal. If your intention is to get a good grade on a test, having achieved the optimal physical and psychological state, begin to feel, see, and hear yourself finishing the test with confidence. Imagine what it would feel like to get the grade you want. What are other people around you saying? What are you saying to yourself? Where are you located and what are you doing? Is it bright, dark, loud, quiet? To make it personal, try adding people that can help you or that you greatly admire into the scene. Work and play with the image/movie until it is superbly fine-tuned to maximize the "realness" of the intention.

4. Let it Go: Finally, as you hold this perfect/ideal scene of the desired outcome in your mind, imagine letting it go out into the world. By letting it go, you are practicing non-attachment and releasing expectation.

It is important to experiment and be playful with this process to find out what works best for you. My optimal process is to form an image, give it motion, add people, make it larger than life, and put myself into the scene as I look down onto it. As I do this, I assess the "realness" of the constructed image by the quality and strength of feelings and sense of movement within my body. This process gives me a sense of power and control over my destiny, adding to my self-worth, confidence, and ability to succeed in the world.

3

The Journey of Being Numb

It's funny how looking back I see all these clues that I missed....

So I left

Now What?

Moving into my parents' home was an emotional task for me to do.

I felt like a complete failure.

A failure at having a successful marriage

A failure at adulting because I returned to the bedroom I grew up in.

A failure at saving what I thought was true love.

I was so hard on myself when I first separated from Best Friend.

At first I attempted to continue counseling services in hope that I could make sense of it all. But nothing made sense, so I stopped going after two weeks.

The first month of me returning to my parents' house I cried myself to sleep every night.

You know, the silent sobbing because the walls are so thin and you don't want anyone to know you're hurting and that you feel broken, so you muffle all your tears and pain in your pillow.

I was always a pro at hiding my feelings. Masking joy or pain didn't matter. I never wanted people to know what I felt.

I UNDERSTAND WHY

I guess I was fearful of being mocked or judged or even spoken about behind my back.

It's crazy because years later here I am sharing my private thoughts and hardships. Exposing parts of my life that I was so ashamed of.

But that's the thing… Being divorced is nothing you should feel ashamed of. No one knows what you were going through behind closed doors. Let spectators do the only thing they will ever be good at, which is not having a fulfilling life of their own so they have to weigh in on yours.

I let my divorce take away my power. I had to fight hard to get this power back, and I want the same for you.

It's funny how life can change you.

Beat you up so bad just to toughen you up.

So there I was on this journey of getting to know this new version of myself. Getting to know what I like and don't like. Trying out new adventures, doing things I always wanted to do, but was too afraid.

This worked at first. Hiding behind different new hobbies and staying occupied in various situations so that I would be so busy I wouldn't have time to think. I remember telling myself, *I'll deal with all my real emotions when I get my own place*. I made up a whole excuse to how living in my parents' house wasn't the best place to truly heal because I didn't have any privacy. I continuously told myself, *When I get my own place I will deal with my unresolved issues*.

I was able to put off my healing for a year, but I had to pay up eventually. My due date was November 2, the day that I purchased my condo. The day started out fine. I was excited to sign all the paperwork, as trying to get my condo had been a headache and a half.

My journey to getting my condo was a special journey. In a way I feel like it introduced me to how to manifest things into my life. I prayed on getting this condo for five months. The first issue was that the condo was way out of my price range, so I started looking elsewhere, but always checked to see if any other condos in the complex would become available. I would check realtor.com daily, and finally I saw that the same condo I wanted had dropped $75,000.

I had my realtor reach out and set up a day for me to visit the condo before I made any decision. My realtor told me that she was able to get in contact with the owner's realtor and that I would be able to visit the condo the following week, but there was an issue. The current tenants weren't ready to move out and had been giving everyone a hard time about coming into the condo. I told my realtor I still wanted to check out the condo, and so we met up on the scheduled date and time. I remember knocking and waiting with no one answering the door, but you could hear the voices in the home. We knocked and rang the doorbell until a lady answered. At first she was hesitant and didn't want us to come in, but eventually she gave in. Once we entered the condo we walked around, and I fell in love. The home looked a mess but I wasn't worried about it because I knew I was renovating that home before I ever would move in anyways, and I just knew that this condo was mine.

Before we even walked out of the building I told my real estate agent to put in the bid. My real estate agent and mom, who'd joined me on my house hunt, looked at me confused. They couldn't understand why I would want that condo, but I didn't care; it felt like home. It was a two story condo with two bathrooms and two bedrooms with a loft. The condo had a beautiful view of the waterfront under the Staten Island Bridge

I UNDERSTAND WHY

which at night lights up and in the darkness of the night the lights shine into the master bedroom window. I was in love. Yeah, it needed a lot of TLC, but that was fine. Because I knew that there was more to the condo than met the eye. I saw other available condos in the building that had an upgraded look, and they were gorgeous. So I knew once I got everything redone, my place would look just as nice.

Once my realtor put in the bid, we were told that the condo was already in the process of being sold to a different family. My heart sank, and I felt defeated, but for some reason I continued to look on realtor.com every day and would still see the same condo up for sale. So eventually I told my realtor to reach out again, and she said she did and was informed that there may be a possibility that the previous family wouldn't be able to move in because they were having a hard time selling their current home.

Eventually the real estate agent of the owner contacted me and told me that the condo was available and that they were going to accept my offer. I was excited! I started filling out all the paperwork and was waiting on the signed documentation from the owner, but after a month it never came. When my real estate agent contacted the owner's realtor, we were informed that there was a mix-up in the paperwork and the realtor signed over the condo to a "different Tiffany." I was pissed, but not defeated. I remember driving out to the waterfront and sitting under a light pole staring into the water. I would go out there almost every day, as it was summertime, and the weather was nice. I would sit out there and pray. I would walk around the community and claim my condo.

Then there was one day where I received a phone call from a Caribbean lady who said she was the owner's realtor and that the error was corrected, and the condo could be mine if my realtor agent sent over all the signed documents again. I reached out to my realtor and we started the process again.

Two months later I found myself at a meeting with my realtor, the previous condo owner, and a whole bunch of other people, and I was signing the paperwork to become an official homeowner. I was ecstatic.

That same night I met up with my contractor at Home Depot and started purchasing all the supplies that I had already picked out. I needed the floors, the light fixtures, the paint color, etc. I was on a mission to make my home feel brand new.

I was on a roll, but somehow while at Home Depot, everything changed. I felt my chest caving in. I couldn't breathe. I was having a panic attack, but why?

This feeling of complete overwhelm lingered for weeks. I had to take some time off from my jobs to catch my breath and try and relax, but nothing worked.

Eventually I went to a therapist.

I remember sitting in my second session explaining all my symptoms and feelings. I complained about my love life, as I was in an on-again, off-again situationship for about a year.

Finally, my therapist told me, "Tiffany, your body is telling you to pay up."

"You ran from dealing with the pain of your divorce... These anxiety attacks have nothing to do with your current situation; these attacks are due to your unresolved past."

It was a year and a half after my divorce, and my body was still holding on to the hurt and pain.

I don't think I even realized how traumatic my divorce really was.

I always thought if I just turned my focus onto different projects in my life, then the pain from the divorce would just go away. I also thought if I dated then that also meant that I was over everything I went through during my marriage, but once again I was wrong.

During my time receiving therapy, I learned and finally understood the importance of taking time out for yourself after a divorce. I also learned that it was okay for me to get a divorce. I believe I carried so much uncertainty with me due to outsiders' opinions. When I went through my divorce I was torn... I saw so many advocates of marriage but no advocates of love and most importantly self-love. I thought all these marriage coaches were right in their statements telling me and other vulnerable women to stay in there and work it out, but here's the thing—for me they were WRONG! I tried everything to avoid divorce, but after I realized fighting for my marriage was literally affecting my mental and physical health, I had to leave. Even after making the choice to leave my marriage, I doubted myself, which was not based on the reasons I left but instead based on outsiders telling me over and over again that I have to suffer through hell and eventually things will get better ... I needed an advocate for people who decided the best thing for them is to leave... or even if the decision was made for you how to deal with moving on.

So because I felt there wasn't a big representation for females who needed an advocate like I needed, I thought I should be that advocate.

During my healing process, I researched topics from how to heal from a broken heart to how to manifest your destiny, and I wrote down all the steps that I took to help me become the best version of myself.

My transformation began when I realized "It's my life, and I am not going to let anyone take control of it; I am the one in charge!" When I started to finally allow myself to heal, I learned so much about myself. One of the things I learned was I had lost myself way before I even got married. My rebuilding process was a struggle, but being honest with myself, healing, and forgiving brought so much peace and fulfillment into my life.

MY 5-STEP FORMULA

These steps are designed to support you in releasing the pain, guilt, shame, and disappointment of the past.

Acknowledge

Embrace

Accept

Forgive

Love Yourself

In taking these steps you'll get:

1. Peace through forgiveness
2. Understanding where you are and what matters to you now
3. Rediscovering who you are as an individual
4. Getting a clearer idea on what direction you want your life to go in
5. Reconnecting and discovering what your needs and desires are and moving toward them

I UNDERSTAND WHY

ACKNOWLEDGE:

I think somewhere down the line after my divorce from Best Friend I rushed into dating again to hide from my feelings. I had to be honest with myself and understand that I loved him and it had hurt me to walk away. I tried so hard to act like I was good. I tried to convince myself that I didn't need a break for my heart to heal.

I also had to admit and acknowledge that I was not wrong for getting my divorce and I needed time to heal before dating again. I carried so much guilt with me, and it showed. For me my guilt of letting go of my marriage showed through me fighting for a situationship that wasn't necessary to fight for. I was determined to make me and this man—let's call him "Woulda Coulda Shoulda"—work out and I truly didn't understand why.

Ladies, have you ever been with someone who didn't treat you right, made you cry over and over again by telling lies and being deceitful, and you were just so blinded by everything that the choices that you make to stay and continue to deal with the pain don't even make sense to you? Well that's where I was. It was crazy; I was acting completely out of character 99 percent of the time because unknowingly part of me just wasn't ready to take another L. Part of me felt like I had walked away from my marriage too easily, and I somehow convinced myself that this relationship was going to be different. I was going to make this work PERIOD.

Sounds crazy, I know, but that's exactly how I know looking back now how much in denial I was. I couldn't even think clearly.

EMBRACE:

After I took the time to acknowledge that my divorce from Best Friend was not just something I could sweep under the rug, I then did the one thing I was truly afraid to do. I allowed myself to feel all the pain. I allowed my heart to hurt without trying to fight off any emotions. Now this phase was not easy at all. It felt like the divorce had just happened. I had to allow myself to mourn, and even though I had cried when I first left Best Friend, I downplayed a lot of my pain. Now I had my own place where the ugly truth about how I felt was able to be revealed. Almost two years later, I was finally tapping into my healing process.

ACCEPTANCE:

On this journey of wanting to rebuild myself, I was determined to be completely honest with myself. My rebuilding process was not just about healing from the divorce, but also what changes I could make to be the best version of myself. So I decided to take the time and write down what I felt my flaws and shortcomings were in the relationship and in my overall life. I know no one wants to point out their flaws, and it is always so easy to see and point out the errors of others, but honestly how does pointing out only the errors of others help you? Let your ex handle their shit, and you take care of your own. Because if you like it or not, you've got flaws and errors too, and if you want to move your life into a place of peace and happiness and become the best version of yourself, that takes being real with yourself.

I UNDERSTAND WHY

FORGIVENESS:

I would have to say this step was the hardest for me. One day I took the time to truly look at myself in the mirror and see beyond my outward appearance. What I saw in the mirror was a scared little girl who thought she wasn't smart enough. I saw an angry woman because she was sexually abused in her past and had never fully healed. I saw a female who wasn't sure if she knew what love was and didn't think she was deserving of it. All these different versions of myself I saw, and I didn't like them.

I first worked through my issues of forgiving myself for all the negative self-talk I'd made myself endure throughout the majority of my life. I did this by reciting positive affirmations. I know it sounds corny, but believe me when I tell you you have to feed yourself with uplifting and positive thoughts until you truly start to feel and believe them. One of the ways I did my positive affirmations was when I joined a kickboxing gym. Everytime I hit the bag, I let out a positive affirmation. It was emotional for me, and it hurt to even admit some of my negative self-talk, but it was time to switch up my mindset. At first I would go to the gym and work on two affirmations at a time. I would say, "I am smart" and "I deserve to be happy" with every hit and kick to the bag. It was like somehow I was releasing all the hurt and pain I'd held on to all my life. It was needed and it worked. Affirmations, journaling, and being real with myself was a big part of my forgiveness and healing process.

Next, I had to realize that I needed to forgive Best Friend. I held anger toward him for not meeting me halfway. I had to realize that Best Friend had his own journey and story, and he had his own issues he had to work out.

After forgiving Best Friend, I had to work on forgiving a piece of my childhood. There was someone in my life that I had to call and have an overdue conversation with. Let's call this person Storm. Storm was a family friend who I still had to be around from time to time. Storm and I never talked about our past situation in full detail, but I felt like I was holding on to the pain that I felt as a child, and I didnt want to carry that hurt and anger anymore. I called Storm one night and told them that I wanted to talk about our past. Storm explained to me their side of the story and apologized for hurting me, as it was not the intention. I felt like forgiving Storm was needed, but that wasn't the only thing that I needed. I also set some boundaries with Storm. For whatever reason, they were still someone I would run into from time to time. Each time hugs were given, and I hated it. While forgiveness was important for me, the most important thing I did in the conversation was take back my power. I set up healthy boundaries about what I am okay with and what I am not okay with. Eventually Storm asked me if I never wanted to be around them again, and I gave my honest answer.

Setting up healthy boundaries and forgiving Storm lifted such a heavy burden that I had carried throughout my life and which also played a role in my relationships. I knew that if my goal was to become the best version of myself, I needed to regain my voice and my power. And that is exactly what I did.

LOVE ON THY SELF:

After working through all my steps—which took a long time—I was finally in a position that I had a clear vision of who I was, and I loved it. Through my healing process I learned so much about myself. The number one thing that I learned is that I am a force to be reckoned with. If you could speak with anyone that knew the hurt version of my past, they would tell you I was timid and shy. After releasing all my fears, hurt and pain, and truly loving on myself, I was able to grow into the *try me if you want badass female I* always knew I was.

As I lived my life with no apologies, my dating life also started to move a little differently. I was no longer putting up with the dumb games.

It's funny because I had a few people try and come back in the picture—including Best Friend.

One of the people that also attempted to come back in my life was Woulda Coulda Shoulda.

I ran into Woulda Coulda Shoulda at the mall, and by the end of the night I received a text from him.

> Woulda Coulda Shoulda: Hey Tiff, it was nice seeing you earlier. You've been on my mind… I would love to take you out for lunch.
> Me: Hey stranger… lunch would be nice.

The backstory to me and this man was Woulda Coulda Shoulda and I were never anything more than a situationship. You know, talking but not making the title for a full-blown relationship official, and me foolishly giving him access to me as though he was my man. It wasn't because I didn't want to be with him officially, but he used to give me every excuse as to why he wasn't ready for a committed relationship. Oh, I was so naïve back then.

When I tell you this man had me open and all in my feelings back when we used to talk, it hurt like hell when we finally parted ways.

I missed him.

I thought I loved him. Like I said, I was so naïve back then.

This man didn't even see fit to make us official, but I settled for the scraps that were given to me.

I would call, and he wouldn't respond.

I would text, and he wouldn't text back until days later.

I was drained by him.

All we did was go back and forth on why we couldn't be in an official relationship for a year straight.

But nonetheless I still took him up on his offer for a lunch date.

We met up at a little spot in the city for lunch three days later.

Everything was going fine at first. We laughed and reminisced about our time together. I talked about my goals and aspirations and how I was planning on opening my second business soon. Our conversion just flowed effortlessly.

After the light talk and reminiscing, Woulda Coulda Shoulda made a comment that made me look at him in a different light.

"You know, Tiffany, you're the one."

He put down his fork and stared at me.

"I just wish I would have noticed this sooner."

"Everything happens for a reason," I answered.

"I just wish I Woulda known so I Coulda handled things better the way I Shoulda."

Yes, that's why his name is Woulda Coulda Shoulda.

"What do you mean?" I asked, confused.

"You know, I wish I Woulda known how you felt about me... you Coulda been my lady, and that's why I asked you out for lunch. I want to make things right, the way it Shoulda been. You know, turn you into my lady. I didn't want to admit it back then, but I love you."

I UNDERSTAND WHY

Woulda Coulda Shoulda went on and told me all the things he liked about me and how he felt like I was the one that got away.

I sat there in disbelief. I couldn't believe the way he casually said he felt he was now ready to turn me into his lady almost a year after we ended our time together.

I remember sitting at the table and thinking to myself this man done lost his ever-loving mind. All of the sudden I had a flood of memories of me crying and begging this man from when we used to talk.

Then I thought to myself
Of course he would want to get with me.
I'm a great person, funny, caring, and nurturing,
I work hard.
I'm running my business and talking about my goals and aspirations.
I'm a bomb-ass chick.

….But then it finally clicked and I had to ask myself this question: *What is something he mentioned to me today that makes him deserving to be even considered a candidate to become my man?*

The answer to that was *Not a damn thing!*

I was so caught up in my thoughts I guess it showed on my face because Woulda Coulda Shoulda was shouting my name by the time I put my focus back to the nonsense he was speaking.

"Tiffany, Tiffany, you there?"

I laughed and answered, "Yeah, I'm here."

Then I looked him in his eyes and said,

"I understand why you would want me, but why would I want you?"

And that was the game changer.

4

Start A New Life

Once you have digested the fact that your entire life is going to change, something odd happens. Unless your partner has died, when this is predictable, you may be surprised to find out that you are in mourning. This is not so surprising if you have lost your partner to death. Even though that is way harder to live through, everyone expects you to be grieving. They may be a little surprised when every single emotion from losing someone you love to death is suddenly in play in your separation or divorce.

There is a reason this is listed near the top of human stressors. Aside from the obvious—you have just lost your best friend, companion and lover, your finances have been altered drastically and almost overnight, you may very well have learned that you will need to relocate—your friends may feel uncomfortable, some will be judgmental even, and the support system that you enjoyed as a couple has now dwindled to nothing at all. It's you against the world.

Betrayal may have been a part of your decision to become single again. If so, you may also temporarily feel unattractive, undesirable, and unwilling to re-enter the dating scene. This is a major change in your life.

If crying feels like the most pressing emotion, do it frequently. It is God's way of clearing the energy field! Sooner or later, the tears dry up. Follow any grief group and you will learn that the next emotion you will feel is anger. These are all powerful emotions and are fairly consuming. This is an emotional roller coaster ride. It is simply the same process of grieving; something has died.

If your spouse truly has died, each emotional stage will be even stronger. There is little or no hope for a healing or better outcome from that loss; there will be no other chance to say what you meant or what you wished you had said; it's over.

Somewhere between the first tears you need to pull your head out of your heartbeat and separate the emotion from the facts. This is the only way you will be equipped to make good decisions.

It is unfortunate that humans are forced to deal with the almighty dollar just between the first sets of tears. This is the reason you must use your head and not your heart. It is necessary if you want to emerge somewhere close to intact.

If a death is involved, you have the obvious final arrangements, insurance claims to file, Social Security to file for, notifications on joint property and credit cards... life gets really busy the first two weeks after losing a partner to death.

Once you have handled the banking issues and notified the credit card companies, make sure you have adequate legal representation unless you have settled on dissolution with everything in agreement.

Regardless of the discussion you may have had when you agreed to end your relationship, don't assume that your partner is still your best friend or anything else you can count on. If you have found someone else, remember it takes time to build a new relationship like that.

Your next step is closely and honestly examining finances. You may decide that you need to move to adjust from the loss of income from your partner. If that is the only option and you own your home or condo, put the castle up for sale; if you are renting or leasing, see what is involved in being released from the lease or rental agreement.

You can actually get excited in a new space; it is not filled with memories and sorrow.

You may discover that your perfectly furnished home now looks like a flea market just before the final closing day. Everything is picked over as it was separated. Nothing looks the same. Find some helpful tips on relocating and making your new house a home. It may be worth a review.

Every time something else changes, you may feel an overwhelming sense of sadness. Go with it. This is natural and normal, and you will recover much quicker if you just allow yourself to feel it. If you don't feel these things, you may learn that your relationship was over long before you called the game.

You just have to make your own way through this process; keep any thoughts of malice and revenge at bay. Emotion is a hook that will catch you in situations you don't want to be in and focus your energy in places that will not promote good results. They will only bring more heartbreak regardless of what you may think at the time. Remember, think with your head, not your heart; it's probably broken right now anyway.

I discovered that if you attempt to rush out and replace this loss of companionship immediately, you will find yourself with a replica of what you just left... times 10. Give yourself some time to get to know the new you; you have probably gotten a little older and a lot wiser in this process. Learn to love yourself before getting involved with anyone else to love.

I consider spouses, parents, children, and siblings to be the biggies in life. Regardless of how bad this ending feels, this is a part of your life plan. Go with the flow. It is very likely that you have a better match lined up at a higher level. Don't assume this is the end of all things good. It may be the beginning of all things great! A little faith goes a long, long way in this situation.

I also learned a little trick... If this has been particularly painful to you, and everywhere you look all you see is the face of the person who has just left, find a ridiculous cartoon that makes you laugh in spite of yourself; then insert your partner's face into the characters. Laughter is a tremendous healing salve to open wounds.

This too shall pass; you just need to survive the process. Find something to be thankful about this situation and stop and be thankful every day, several times a day. This kind of energy ushers in the next best part of our life in a very positive and uplifting way.

Make some generic friends and acquaintances and enjoy their company.

Recently an old collegue visited me. It had been many, many years since we had communicated. She was now divorced, but I had associated with her and her husband some years back.

She had survived a marriage of twenty plus years fraught with trauma and turmoil, including lying, cheating, and abuse. Finally, she told me, she had escaped! Or had she?

He had fallen for a recently widowed neighbor who had inherited a lot of money. In her great anger, my friend spent $26,000 on a divorce attorney to make him pay for the years and years of abuse he had tortured her with!

She had gone to court and won a really large monthly alimony. She had fixed him! She began a new life based on that court order. Soon he began dragging her back to court, a common occurrence that had spanned more than nine years when I saw her. In an effort to 'get back at her,' he quit his job of 20 years, took menial positions or none at all, and soon reduced her monthly alimony to barely over $400.00.

She lost everything, over and over. She won his pension, spent it, and was on the streets again. A trail of misery and disillusionment was firmly in place. She had finally gotten yet another settlement and had purchased a condo. But he was taking her back to court again in a few weeks; she was afraid of losing her $400.00, her only income, and then the condo, the only roof over her head, again.

She told me this had been going on for nine years! She could not stop talking about all that he had taken from her; he had driven her health to decline and caused her to have two nervous breakdowns.

She believed she could no longer work and earn an income that would help maintain her new life. She feared she would have another breakdown.

On and on she went with the stories of what he had done to her. She was deeply enmeshed in affording him the power to destroy her life. He had nearly succeeded; or she had.

I looked her in the eyes and asked her why? "Why is he so important? How did he gain the power to destroy you? He was not a particularly good catch when you had him!" He sure did not have those kinds of power over her future then. Why now?

I know some people judge and doubt how something as painful as a relationship can be the cause of having a nervous breakdown on two occasions and permit a perfectly sane and capable woman to have lost all that she was before the divorce.

Rather than choosing to be responsible for the abuse she had chosen to accept for more than twenty years, she committed to making him pay; she became the piper. All of her life energy and emotions were swept into this cause. She lost her way on her path of life and endured many more painful years even after her divorce was final. She had now spent nearly thirty years tied to this delusion that she was in control and could make him pay. This had taken a terrible toll on her and was reflected in her life.

Her absolute refusal to let go and release herself from this situation had caused her incredible pain, filled her with debilitating fear that he would take even more away, and robbed her of the opportunity to bring far more joy and light into her life.

I always assumed there is a lesson for me when I see things like this in someone who suddenly appears on the horizon after years of separation. There always is: let the hell go! Stop holding on to the pain; like the tiger, it does not change its stripes. No matter how long you hold on, it delivers the same blunt force trauma as the first time. It is not a familiar friend; let go!

Nothing in life is worth paying this high of a price. Step into your new life fearlessly; confidence follows fearless footsteps.

HOW TO MANIFEST YOUR OWN DESTINY WITH EASE

How to manifest your own destiny—what is the secret? There is an absolute truth to the age-old saying "You can do whatever you can put your mind to." Every person who has satisfyingly manifested a goal has started with a seedling thought, which merges into a desire, and then through focus, commitment, and perseverance reformed their desire into the real world.

WRITE DOWN YOUR GOALS

To manifest your own destiny, you must be absolutely certain about what your goals are. No component is insignificant if it adds to your inner experience and the feeling of having what you want. Write down in clear and precise detail exactly what you desire. By documenting your goals, your mind carries out a 'mini-visualization' and constructs a mental picture which it links to your goal. Your desire must be written in the present-day tense using an affirmative slant. For example: "It is August 2021, and I have $20,000 saved towards my home deposit" rather than "I am going to save money for my home deposit." Positively direct what you are saying, thinking, and feeling towards your aspiration, and ensure that it is positioned as closely as possible to your innermost core standards.

FOCUS ON YOUR GOAL

To create your ultimate reality you have to have your heart set on it, be totally committed and focused, and never give up on the belief that it is yours—continue to believe that your dream will be fulfilled. The instant you commit to an intention to manifest a specific thing, the universe has already created it; however, you have to maintain a constant focus before it can be realized in your life. As per the Law of Attraction, the energy vibration that is diffused from our thoughts embodies itself and is magnetically drawn toward a congruent vibration. The things in your life that you choose to repeatedly concentrate your attention and thoughts on will be magnetically drawn toward your vibration and will manifest in your reality.

Keep being an amazing woman! Visualize your goal.

I UNDERSTAND WHY

Use your imagination and create a picture in your brain of your objective. This is a wonderful method for speeding up the manifesting process. If you find it hard to create a snapshot in your mind, then assemble an assortment of appropriate photos in a scrapbook or a PowerPoint presentation and spend between ten to thirty minutes concentrating your focus on your dream. To improve the effectiveness of this process, ensure that you incorporate the use of all five senses if possible. By including sound, touch, sight, smell, and taste, your visualization experience will be enhanced.

BELIEVE

Within your soul you must believe that what you desire is yours right now—feel the excitement of achieving your goal. When you are visualizing your goals, imagine that it is already in your reality. Don't ponder "how" your goal is going to come about; just trust that you have put your order in, and it is on its way. Our universe is infinitely abundant, and anything you desire is possible. Just believe it to be so in the present moment.

By understanding the principles of the Law of Attraction, you begin to comprehend that anything and everything is possible. The true essence of life is our tremendous ability to manifest, and we all have this incredible skill. The simple fact is YOU were born to manifest miracles!

INCREASE SELF-LOVE

One of the most common questions I hear from clients is this:

EVERYONE KEEPS TELLING ME TO "LOVE MYSELF" BUT WHAT DOES THAT LOOK LIKE AND HOW DO I DO IT?

I'll begin with my favorite quote on self-love, which comes from Lucille Ball:

> *"Love yourself first and everything else falls into line. You really have to love yourself to get anything done in this world."*

I couldn't agree more with her on this one. However, her quote doesn't offer any clues about how to love oneself in the first place. I'm not going to pretend that there is some quick and easy answer to this daunting question, but I have put a lot of time, thought, and study into this particular question, so I'll offer up some of what I've learned here...

THREE FAST WAYS TO INCREASE SELF-LOVE

#1: REALIZE THE INCREDIBLE BENEFITS OF SELF-LOVE

There are a multitude of excellent reasons to extend compassion and love toward ourselves as well as others. In a nutshell, I've learned that everything we are trying to achieve becomes a whole lot easier and less stressful when we are kind toward ourselves, rather than harsh and critical.

I UNDERSTAND WHY

Here Are Some Benefits of Self-Love

- We let go of blame, shame, and anger. We invite ownership, creation, and power into our lives.
- The more we look at ourselves with love, the more we practice love and acceptance toward others.
- We allow ourselves to be human. We accept mistakes and failures, and we invite vulnerability into our lives.
- We let go of competition and comparing ourselves to others.
- We find courage to accept failure because we know that it is one step closer to growth, and our significance isn't dependent on what we produce.

#2: EXTEND COMPASSION TOWARD YOURSELF

I was sitting with a lovely client who has a terrible habit of beating herself up emotionally. I'm guessing you can relate to this... I sure can! It appeared that she was trying to convince me (or herself?) that she was basically a "hopeless case" and not worthy of living a rich, juicy, and fulfilling life because she had an eating disorder which had plagued her for the last ten years.

She would probably make a great lawyer, as she is incredibly adept at making a case. The only problem in my opinion is that her case is against HERSELF. And if anything is going to interfere with one's capacity to experience self-love, freedom, and living a fantastic life, I'd say, hands down, it's when you beat yourself up emotionally regularly and consistently. And let me tell you, this beautiful young woman is not the only one guilty of this.

Unfortunately, I sit with countless women, either face to face, on the phone, or via video-conferencing who tell me exactly why they don't deserve a crack at happiness. The reasons given could be one or all of the following:

- Any one or more of these conditions: Divorce trauma, anxiety, depression, eating disorders, addictions, ADHD, etc.
- Past history of abuse
- A history of bad choices
- Not being where they are "supposed to be" at this point in their life

And more...

So as I sat listening to this woman berate herself mercilessly, something came to me. As she finished each reason for hating herself and not deserving a great life, I finished her sentence with, "And yet, I still love myself." At first, she looked really annoyed that I was interrupting her, but as I continued playfully ending her sentences, a smile broke out on her lips, and she started to laugh. We laughed and enjoyed the fun dance we were doing together.

After a while, she stopped talking and looked me squarely in the eyes and said, "That is really helpful. I suppose if I can have all these problems and still love myself despite them, I wouldn't be so upset at myself all the time PLUS have all of these problems."

Very wise words indeed. Isn't it bad enough that we have these problems to begin with? Why do we have to add insult to injury by beating ourselves up emotionally as well? When are we going to give ourselves a break by saying to ourselves when we falter, "And yet, I still love myself." Give it a try and see what happens.

I UNDERSTAND WHY

#3: CHANGE YOUR SELF-TALK

For the final suggestion on how to love yourself more, I can't stress enough the importance of how you talk to yourself. Research has found that we practise self-talk for FOUR HOURS every day, so be mindful of how you use those four hours! I can take a guess that the majority of us are incredibly cruel to ourselves during this big chunk of the day, during which time the harsh inner critic comes out and berates us constantly for not being _____ enough. This blank space is often one of a long list. Here are the most common ones I hear from clients:

- Smart
- Thin
- Sexy
- Funny
- Rich
- Charming
- Pretty
- Kind
- Young

You can probably add one or two of your own variations to the list. However, I think it would be far more productive to start switching the negatives to positives when you catch yourself being mean to yourself.

Life after divorce starts with YOU. Getting YOU back. Losing your identity is so common and overlooked by us women that we tend to lose sight of it. Changing your perspective is key. Reevaluate the situation, not what you could have done differently, but what BOTH of you could have done differently. Acceptance is the hard part after divorce, but you will get to that point soon enough.

Remember, it was not your fault. Granted, no one is perfect. I am sure you have made some mistakes along the way, just like I am sure I have as well. But don't dwell on that. Dwell on now, and the fact that you landed on this page tells me you want healing. You want answers. My friend, healing is available. Talk to God and pray, give yourself time, and allow yourself to feel the pain. It is part of the healing process. Grab some pillows and scream into them, punch some punching bags if you have to ... Let it out! You will feel better once you do that.

Give yourself credit because you will make it. Life after divorce is not as bad as people may make it seem. It may be scary at first, but nine times out of ten, you will grow into an even more phenomenal woman than you already were!

Even if your relationships haven't suffered yet, you will notice an improvement in them as your other intentions get manifested.

Once you set your intentions, take a few minutes each day to visualize each one of them. And then put all of them together by creating a story in your mind. Use your imagination. Add feeling to your visualization, as if the scene in your mind had already happened. Carry these intentions in your mind everywhere you go, and be attentive to your surroundings. Look for synchronicities. Opportunities to act on certain things will pop up seemingly out of nowhere. It's the Universe at large acting on your behalf. It's the genie you saw in "The Secret." Take inspired action if you feel like it. Do not judge or try to see how this or that wouldn't work. Just do it and have faith. Before you know it, your intentions will start materializing in front of your eyes!

But don't stop there. To achieve a balanced life you must have intentions in every aspect of your life at all times. If you already have your ideal job, now set an intention to get a promotion as soon as possible. Or if you have the home of your dreams, set an intention to get that plasma TV you so much want... you get the idea. Keep on moving, and the Universe will back you up.

I UNDERSTAND WHY

MANIFESTING YOUR SOUL MATE

There are a few things to consider in your manifesting work. Before you manifest something into your life, think about how you're going to feel when you get it. For instance, I had a friend once who led a life of loneliness and rejection for many years. He had been overweight most of his life and had not been successful in love. However, his life changed. He lost weight and got in great shape, and it completely changed his life. Once these things happened, John set an intention to have a trophy wife. He talked about it all the time. He may not have been consciously manifesting... because at that time he had no idea what it meant to manifest something into your life. However, he was successful; he met and married very quickly a beautiful young woman who was simply stunning. He seemed to be so happy that his dream had come true. I saw him a year later and he told me that he and his wife had divorced. As it turned out, he said she lacked the moral character he desired in a mate, and she had been unfaithful to him after running up nearly $40,000 in credit card debt. He sat down and rubbed his head and said, "You know Tiffany, I just don't know what went wrong."

What went wrong is that John got what he asked for. He manifested this person into his life. Be careful what you ask for.

So step one is to review your soul mate description and consider how step three felt to you. When you imagined your life with this person in it... did you take into consideration all aspects of what your soul mate will bring to the table? Make sure you have covered all the bases. I also think it's relevant to consider the motivation behind your desires. Is your motivation pure? Are you seeking to find this soul mate to feed your spirit and share your journey so that you can live life with intention and purpose, bringing good to the world together? Are your desires spirit driven or ego driven? It's helpful to write down the reasons you desire this person in your life. Desires from the ego seldom serve us.

Now that you have considered your desires and motivation carefully, let's get started honing your manifesting tools. Follow these steps to help you achieve the actualization of your perfect partner.

1. Believe!! You have set an intention... now believe he/she is coming.
2. Meditation - take time daily to connect to your spirit and get grounded. By doing so you will be more inspired to live in the anticipation of your partner and take actions from integrity.
3. Clean up - Remember that what you have been doing is not working. So make changes... begin to create and develop the life you want to live with your soul mate. Eliminate things that are not serving you and your purpose and that are not in alignment with your intentions and desire. Focus instead on things that will serve you and your partner in the wonderful life you are going to build together.
4. Build it and they will come! Create a space for you new life and your new partner. How will they come if there is no room in your life for them? Make your home ready to welcome your soul mate! Do you have a bedside table on both sides of your bed? Is it free of clutter and inviting? Do you have a special place for him/her to relax in your home... you have your favorite chair you like to relax in... is there a space for him

to do the same? Get out both of your coffee cups and have a second robe waiting. Make time in your life for your new partner, and put yourself in the presence of his/her energy frequently. Connect with them.

5. And perhaps the most important step of all... make yourself ready. Love and cherish your body and take care of it. Perhaps you need a new look to go along with your new life and partner. Ask yourself is your wardrobe up to date, are you due a stylish new haircut, are you engaged in self-care both physically and mentally? Be at your best!! Get a mini makeover if you need it. Enjoy the process... remember part of manifesting your soul mate is making yourself ready.

6. Create a ritual of invitation... Write a letter to your soul mate inviting them into your life... tell them you have created a wonderful space in which to share an extraordinary life with them. Tell your partner in the letter that you are waiting for them and welcome them. Wish them Godspeed on their journey to you! Now burn the letter and as the smoke rises into the skies and spreads in all the directions of the universe, send out your intentions with it.

7. Be grateful... be grateful for your journey. Be grateful for all the experiences in your life that have led you to where you are today. Be grateful for your soul mate, who is seeking you now... and have gratitude that they are on their way.

Unlike the law of gravity, this law is subjective and its effectiveness is determined by several factors. The focus, concentration, clarity of the goal, ability to achieve the optimal state, and ability to let go will greatly affect the results of the manifestation of intent. I like to think of the law of attraction as a process that we all use, every day. Some have greater conscious control over their abilities to manifest, and others wield their power unconsciously.

5

A Breakup to Queen Up Story
Queen Sasha's Story

"Six years, Tiffany."
"Six years of complete bullshit."
"Six years wasted."
"Six years of sacrificing and for what?"

MEET SASHA

Sasha had been divorced for six months when I became her coach, and she was stuck in phase anger.

Sasha and her then husband Terrance were married for six years and had dated for four years prior. During their dating and marriage, they brought two beautiful girls into this world. After Sasha and her husband finally finished the gruesome divorce, where, according to Sasha, she got what she and the kids deserved, and her was-been got what was coming to him, Sasha was still unhappy.

"I did everything for that man.

He stepped out on me while we were dating and I forgave him.

And two years into our marriage, I find out that he is back on this bullshit.

I UNDERSTAND WHY

He was cheating and not even trying to cover his tracks. And what did I do? I stayed!
I stayed….
How could I leave?
We were a family
Those vows I took seriously…
He's a good father—our daughters love him.
I didn't want to leave him. He just checked out
He became cold
Yeah, I was married for six years, but he checked out a long time before we even started talking about leaving one another."

Sasha told me her love story from the beginning to the end. She told me that she and Terrance met during college at a football game. She told me that they wound up pregnant with their first baby girl their second year dating, only one year after they graduated from college and still were trying to figure out their own individual goals and career paths.

"When we first met each other, Tiff, he was everything I thought I needed.

A handsome educated Black man that knew how to treat a woman like a lady.

We were best friends. We told each other our goals and aspirations.

But that second year changed things a little. Adding Makayla into our lives was a blessing but was also very difficult.

We had just graduated college and both moved back to our parents' houses.

I was blessed enough to have been hired through my internship, so I started working in my field right away. Terrance struggled finding the best job for him in his field. He was working in his field but was on entry level and his check matched.

A little after we had Makayla, we decided to move in together, as we wanted to be a family and for our daughter to have access to both of her parents.

A few months after having Makayla, Terrance was caught stepping out on me.

We broke up, but eventually came back together.

When Terrance came back into my life, I swear to you he was a new and improved version of himself.

We were able to pick up our lives back where things left off before he cheated on me. Everything was perfect. So perfect that he asked me for my hand in marriage only eight months after coming back together."

Sasha continued to tell me the joys of her dating life turned marriage and reminisced about all the good times she and her husband had on their journey. She told me that after three years of marriage, they were blessed with another little girl, Ravyn.

"Everything was good in the beginning.

But then ...then something changed.

It wasn't a dramatic overnight change; it was gradual."

With two children, money was a little tight. Sasha said she and Terrance tried to keep the spark in their relationship, but it was hard. Over time they just became more focused on being great parents and slowly let the romance of their relationship slip away.

"Isn't that how it's supposed to be, Tiffany?

I mean, parents have to take care of their children.

We made sure our little girls had everything.

Terrance picked up extra hours at his job.

I came home and did everything that a wife and mother is supposed to do.

I took care of the home..

I UNDERSTAND WHY

I cooked.

I cleaned.

I had sex when he wanted.

I made sure everyone had what they wanted.

And everyone was happy.

But then over time, as Terrance started distancing himself, and the needs of the girls became more demanding, I felt like I was a zombie.

Makayla was on the Victorious Youth dance team and practices were every Monday, Wednesday, and Saturday. And when it was tournament season they added practices on Thursday and tournaments were on Saturday and Sunday.

Don't get me wrong; I'm happy that my little girl was engaged in something that she loved doing.

But between making sure Makayla made it to practice, completed her homework every night, made sure dinner was on the table for everyone no later than 6:30pm, and getting Ravyn on a sleeping schedule, I was exhausted!"

Sasha continued to share how she loved her family and being a mom and wife, but the feeling of being overwhelmed consumed her.

"Yes, Terrance was a great father. He was there for the girls. He supported Makayla at every tournament, but the bulk of the work and responsibility was put on me.

I can never say Terrance was not there for the girls because that would be a complete lie; however, I can say that he was not there for me emotionally.

My relationship with Terrance used to be so effortless, our love was effortless. Over time, somehow our love and relationship started needing effort.

Effort put forth to make time for one another.

Effort put forth to remind each other what we mean to each other.

I tried to express that to Terrance, but he was already checking out.

Terrance took on more hours at work because he said he couldn't concentrate at home with the kids crying, playing, and wanting his attention.

Isn't it interesting when both parents have demanding jobs and sometimes need to put in some work hours at home but one parent has to say no while the other parent gets to do their job to the best of their ability?

I began struggling at work. When I had Ravyn I wasn't able to stay on maternity leave for long because we needed my full check. Trying to find a daycare for Ravyn that didn't take up all our money was also a struggle. But luckily for us, there was a lady at our church that ran a daycare. She was able to help us out with Ravyn, and her prices were reasonable.

When I returned back to work, I struggled. I worked in the HR department and everyone was trying to rise to the top. In my job certs were important, but if you had your masters degree in HR or anything pertaining to business and management, you were way ahead of the game. My goal was to be way ahead of the game.

One late night when Terrance and I were alone in our room, I brought up me going back to school.

'Hey, babe,' I said timidly.

'Yeah?' he yawned while lying with his back to me.

'Remember when we first started dating, we had all these big dreams and goals of killing it at our jobs and being at the top?'

'Yup,' he answered.

'Do you think we got off track?'

'I don't think so. I'm doing great at work and hopefully will be given the next management position when Drew retires at the end of the year.'

'Yeah, I know, babe, and that's great… A position at my job is about to open up, and I'm thinking about applying for it. The pay is great and it requires you to get your masters, which the job will cover a masters degree in HR 100 percent.'

'I don't know, babe. You don't think you'll be taking on too much?'

'What?! No! You know this is what I wanted!' I said, angry and confused.

'I mean, we have a lot on our plates. Between making sure the girls are good and managing both of our work schedules. I think it might be too much…'

I was so pissed that he felt that way. How dare he get to move up the ladder and expect me to just stay put?

I remember getting out of bed and walking to our master bedroom and crying while the water from the faucet ran.

I think a part of me knew my goals were going to have to be put on hold.

Was he right? My job would have had me travel all around the world for various business meetings and conferences. Even trying to go back to school would have been a lot on me. When would I have had the time and energy?

Raising kids takes energy.

You wake up before everyone and you put your kids' needs first, leaving very little time for you to pour into your own needs.

And I was beginning to feel drained."

Sasha continued to explain how she didn't apply for the position and she genuinely didn't think it was a problem until her husband started moving up the ladder at his job and Sasha started feeling resentful and guilty. Then Sasha shared the first time she and her husband got into an argument over him coming home late.

"Where have you been, Terrance?"

"Hey, babe. I was out watching the game at Derrick's," Terrance answered with slurred speech.

"Ugh, you're drunk. Why do y'all like to get drunk every Thursday?"

"I don't know, babe. We just got caught up watching the game. I'm hopping in the shower."

Bling
Bling
Bling
Bling
Bling
Bling

Who's texting him this late? Sasha thought to herself.

"Tiff, have you ever felt like you know some shit is about to go down and rip you from the inside out? That's how I felt. That man's phone went off about 12 times, back-to-back text messages pouring into his phone. So I did what most women would do. I checked it. I didn't care that the messages would show read. I just didn't give a fuck. I had a hunch that something was up.

The second I opened the messages I was crushed. She was texting him. This anonymous female that I kinda knew about but never had any solid proof outside of the scent of perfume on his shirt and light smudges of makeup and lipstick on his shirt and collar. I went so long trying to pretend that it was only a phase for him. Men cheat, right? Men cheat, but they don't leave their wives. I couldn't imagine my life without him, so I never said

I UNDERSTAND WHY

anything. But on this particular night, that all changed. Out of all the messages that flooded his phone there was only one that stood out to me: *This is your baby, it is your responsibility.*

This negroe got his bitch pregnant. I lost it.

Bang bang bang 'Terrance, open up this fucking door now.'

'What the hell is it now, Sasha?' Terrance stood in the bathroom doorway dripping wet.

'What the fuck is this?' I shoved the phone in his face.

Slam.

He grabbed his phone and slammed the door in my face.

That night was the turning point in my relationship.

He left the house after he got out of the shower, and I cried myself to sleep.

I felt numb.

When he finally came back to the house two days later, he made his position very clear.

'Sasha, I don't want to leave you. I slipped up, and that was wrong. I can't say that it won't happen again, but I can say I will try my hardest to keep it from ever getting back to you.'

I was so baffled, hurt, confused, and embarrassed.

I'm not sure how we even got to this point.

It's like he hated me, and I couldn't figure out why.

We started this relationship on love.

We made our daughters out of love.

I did everything a good wife and mother was supposed to do.

We were supposed to be in this together.

How did we get to the point where he no longer had love for me?"

Sasha told me how she stayed in her marriage hoping and praying that it would change. She engaged in counselling and eventually was able to talk her husband into going to marriage counseling with her. No matter her attempts and patience, Terrance continued to be distant. When the marriage counselor gave them assignments to do, Terrance would barely give them much thought, and it showed.

"Okay, Terrance, what was the first thing that you fell in love with about Sasha?" asked the therapist.

"Honestly it was so long ago I don't recall," answered Terrance grumpily.

"Yes, it was a long time ago, which is why you were given a week to think of your answer," stated the therapist.

Terrance stood up and exited the therapist's office. "I don't see the point of this."

Sasha confided to me that she continued to meet with the therapist weekly, updating her on the newest relationship drama, the hidden mistresses, and the constant arguing. By this time in their relationship, Terrance was barely home. He stayed out most nights, not caring about the effect it had on his wife and children. Sasha shared when Terrance would come home all they did was argue. According to Sasha she couldn't do anything right.

"It's crazy that I stayed in that relationship for so long. I felt helpless.

Do I leave?

Do I stay?

I was so torn.

But I think Terrance knew he wanted out.

One night I was trying to put aside all the drama and get us back to where we were.

Sent the kids to my mom's for the night.

I dressed up in some new lingerie.

I UNDERSTAND WHY

Beat my face.
Made sure my hair was on point, and I went out to the living room and danced for him.
See, that's what I used to do back in the day.
He used to love when I gave him dances
And he still liked it, so I thought I had him hooked.
I danced for him and grinded on him, and he carried me to the bedroom.
We had sex—no connection, just sex.
He wouldn't kiss me.
He wouldn't make eye contact with me… It was so long since we were intimate and this is how he did me.
After he was done we laid next to each other and I cried.
I felt disgusting, like I just gave my body up for prostitution.
I don't think he ever made me feel as low as he did in that moment.
'What is it now, Sasha?'
'I can't do this.'
'I deserve better than this.'
'I want a divorce.'
Just like that, those four words slipped off my tongue without a hitch.
That ugly seven-letter word finally caught up to me.
Divorce."

What am I to do?

What am I to do?
Do I ask you to change on behalf of me?
Do I let you continue as you were, knowing that would be the
    end of you and me?

What am I to do?

To change you might mean to lose you.
They say be careful of what you ask for because you never know what you're gonna get.

If you stay the same you will lose me.
Am I willing to leave you and let the next one have everything I put into you?

My happy ending
Where is it?
Starting to think that fairy tales are just fantasy

Always knew I wasn't going to have a happily ever after
But damn we came close

Or didn't we...
Just a few years in wasn't even close to the end
Damn how did I let this happen

The signs I ignored
The truth I embellished
The pain I hid
Happy vs forever
Is that really what I'm left to choose

We can't have it all - one way or the other
I'm afraid to choose
Because I'm going to choose you

Straight ignore my own fears
Drown in my tears
Pretending to be something that we are not

I UNDERSTAND WHY

Have I turned into the person my young self never wanted to be?
If I stay she is exactly who I will be

Stuck
Unhappy
For 10 years straight all I ever wished for was to be happy
I guess I knew what was coming my way
But I still have a chance to escape
I have a chance at happiness
But how?
As a single 30 plus year old woman?
Back on the dating scene?
Wouldn't even know where to start
I'm lost
I thought I was found
I played myself

I believed that I was going to have my shit together
Good job
Happy marriage
Well-behaved kids
Lord, I need guidance

If I let him choose...
He's going to leave me
He always did
Not knowing how to handle his demons from the past he cowards out and loosens his grip on my hand

I walk alone
Lost in the desert

TIFFANY SMITH

Tempted to go back
For what?

She likes her heart broken
She likes the pain put in the songs
It calms her soul
Brings her peace
She understands pain best
Life without pain is foreign
She gonna learn one day
Pain will take her breath away

6

Why Are Breakups So Painful?

We always tend to think that whoever is "left" is the big victim in a relationship. What happens is that whoever is left is in a completely passive situation and is forced to deal with all feelings of helplessness.

It feels like there is nothing you can do. How do you fight to change the person you love to want to continue to grow and love you back?

Those who stay are swept away by a feeling of betrayal, even though there may not have been a "betrayal," properly speaking.

Those who stay feel adrift, abandoned, rejected, unloved ... without a floor. What remains for those left in tears?

Sometimes, depending on the unpreparedness or the surprise with the news, there is an impulse to juggle so that the other will turn back. But it is useless.

What do I mean by juggle? I mean going out of character and doing something you truly don't feel like is you. Sometimes females allow their partners to move as they please, sometimes some females may allow an open relationship even though that may not be what they see as their ideal relationship.

Basically doing anything out of your normal context to say, "Hey look at me! Love me again! Choose me!" is juggling.

I UNDERSTAND WHY

IS THERE A VILLAIN AND A VICTIM?

The mistake is made of believing that whoever left the relationship "is doing well." This is seen as the villain of the story, the one who causes suffering. But that's not how it always happens ...

In a stable relationship, which started with the intention of making it as long as possible, it is clear that both are moving toward solidifying the couple.

It is hoped that love will be forever, and no matter how much you pay attention to the evolution of the relationship, love, lust, the interest in perpetuating the bond can end on one side.

Sometimes it happens that both people in the relationship gradually lose interest and almost at the same time. But in most cases, this disinterest is unilateral.

In some cases, whoever stopped loving is also frustrated. Whoever stopped loving would not like to have stopped loving, but it is not a decision, it just happens.

She searches within herself for a long time to find the desire, the passion of the early days, but finds nothing. She lives a great conflict and mourns.

That She was me. I struggled so much with making the decision to stay or leave due to not wanting to be perceived as the bad guy.

In addition, I felt that I also struggled because society/the church taught me that divorcing was equivalent to giving up. Do you know how many people are out there telling women to stay in there, suffer through, better days are a-coming? But there isn't really an advocate for females to say *You know when enough is enough. I deserve better*. And that leads me to the next topic.

GUILT AND FRUSTRATION

A lady who stopped loving also lost love and may spend a long time blaming herself, anticipating her partner's pain, wanting to prevent him from getting hurt.

And many times, in an attempt to deny that the feelings just faded, in the belief that there must be a more compelling reason for separation, that it is not enough that love and desire have run out, mistakes are made.

If you find yourself in this situation, pay attention not to make the separation unnecessarily more painful than it naturally is, avoiding the following situations:

- Provoke sterile discussions
- Seeking a relationship abroad as a way to punish yourself for guilt for having stopped loving your partner
- Seek forced closeness to "disguise" your real feelings and intentions
- To despise your partner or to treat him with indifference, imagining that this will make him also stop loving you, making your decision easier

Nobody wakes up in the morning with the discovery that they want to part. This is a process; we are gradually realizing ourselves.

Those who go through this experience submit themselves to a distressing reflective recollection because they often cannot easily accept the reality of their feelings.

And until she realizes the impossibility of continuing to live together, the mourning of the loss of a love, of plans, of projects in common is going on.

It is a mistake to believe that anyone who wants to separate "is in good shape." The difference between those who leave and those who stay is that those who leave live in mourning before the effective separation.

And there is added all the courage necessary to communicate to the partner and to manage with balance the developments of that decision.

LITTLE MOURNING

The saying "Never beg for love" is perfectly applicable in cases where the desire to separate is one-sided. When one of the two sides comes to communicate that decision, it has long been matured—and suffered.

The feeling of relief experienced by those who leave and the apparent simplicity with which they can deal with the issue are often seen as insensitivity, and that is another mistake.

Each one in her own way and in her own time lives the pain of loss, and after the first impact, it is always good to keep in mind that in the relationships of affection there is no guarantee certificate and much less expiration date.

Beginning, middle, and end. Even the relationships that last "until death do us part" suffer a small mourning halfway.

HOW TO GET OUT OF A DEPRESSION AFTER A DIVORCE

Divorce is one of the most stressful life events. Acute and chronic stress, especially, affects emotional and physical health. There is research that suggests that divorced people or widows have more chronic diseases (diabetes, cancer ...) by 20 percent than married people. In addition, other studies showed that a person's level of happiness decreases as the divorce approaches, if the person does not work on it.

SYMPTOMS OF DEPRESSION DUE TO DIVORCE

There are cases in which divorce becomes a stressful and traumatic event in which the pain is excessive and some symptoms of depression are experienced:

- Not being able to sleep or sleeping more than normal
- Overeating or lack of appetite
- Excessive fatigue
- Weird and unusual pains
- Excessive consumption of alcohol or drugs
- Difficulty of concentration
- Persistent negative thoughts
- Irritability or anger
- Anxiety or restlessness
- Feeling guilty or worthless
- Pessimism or indifference
- Loss of interest in activities that were previously very rewarding for the person
- Recurring thoughts of death
- Suicidal thoughts (get immediate professional help)

Although it is normal to feel some of these symptoms during this process, you should contact a specialist if you are experiencing at least four of the above symptoms on a day-to-day basis for a prolonged period of time.

FEELINGS AFTER A DIVORCE

From the time you feel there will be a separation, you may go through a series of emotional stages regarding this vital event, usually characterized by pain and loss:

NEGATION

Denial is the way we try to protect ourselves against an "emotional storm" and thus try to overcome emotionally. It is a useful coping mechanism as long as it does not prevent us from leading a normalized life. Therefore, the characteristic of this stage is that it is not abused, that is, we should not remain in denial; refusing to face reality is not an appropriate strategy. Therefore, denial is a useful mechanism in the short term, while in the long term it involves high costs in the person's life.

ANGER

During this stage, the other is blamed for everything that happens to us. For a while, all those adversities that we find in our new life are the fault of the other person; we do not play any role. Anger and pain make us see nothing good in the ex-partner. It is a stage in which any moment is used to release all repressed anger in the denial phase.

NEGOTIATION

This stage is characterized by trying to fix or repair the damage caused by the separation. It is when you stop to think and say, "I cannot deal with this; I will negotiate anything with him/her in order not to go through this."

It is an attempt to recover your "life." At this stage, you begin to miss the positive aspects of the ex-partner, his smile, his jokes ... and you want him to come back. That is, it goes from despising it in the anger stage to weighing it in this negotiation stage. This is where the person debates if the divorce was a right decision or not.

DEPRESSION

At this stage, you will not feel like leaving home or doing anything. You prefer to be in bed or watching TV most of the time. Sadness is your companion during this stage. This is an expected stage throughout this process. Therefore, it is essential that you surround yourself with a good support system, whether family or friends, as well as therapy sessions, if necessary. It is very important not to isolate yourself during this stage.

ACCEPTANCE

This stage is the end. Having passed through adversity, you have overcome it and learned from it, but we must bear in mind that accepting the new situation does not mean that we are always happy and that we do not have negative emotions about divorce.

There may still be times when you feel angry or sad about the loss of your marriage. The important thing is that even if you still have those negative moments or feelings, they are no longer paralyzing or interfering with your life.

TIPS FOR OVERCOMING DIVORCE DEPRESSION

Take note of the following tips that can help you get out of depression after a divorce:

- Don't compare yourself with other people who have been through the same thing as you. Remember that each situation is different and each person is different. In addition, the same situation does not affect us all equally or in the same way.
- Look for new activities and relationships that can help you build your new life, but don't hurry; wait a while before starting to take steps.
- Think of something positive that you can get out of what is happening to you. Every morning before getting up and at night think about something positive of the current moment.
- Do not isolate yourself or live only these difficulties. Lean on your family or friends, but you should choose those people in your environment who have good listening skills and who can respect your feelings and provide support for you.
- Take care of your physical health. Eat healthy, do the physical exercise you can, and try to get enough sleep to maintain good levels of stress and depression.
- Plan activities. Try to do things that in the past were very rewarding, and even if there is sadness or depression, you

must fulfill that plan. It is not about waiting to be well to do things, but to do things to start being well.
- Be aware of your emotions (anger, guilt, sadness, loneliness, etc.) and feel them. The way to free yourself from your emotions is to recognize, accept what you are feeling, and allow yourself to feel them.
- The pain of a separation is not overcome in a day; it is essential to respect the time. There are no adequate times established. Each person has their own circumstances and must mark their times to overcome depression by divorce.

WHAT SHOULD I DO IF I THINK MY RELATIONSHIP IS OVER

Each person is unique, and in the same way, the relationships you have with others are also unique. In this way, it is not good to compare the different situations and circumstances that everyone can live. Although in certain aspects, generalities can be found to take into account.

The reasons that can lead to the end of a marriage are very broad. However, the underlying motive is usually the lack of compatibility, the lack of illusion. In some cases, reasons such as cheating, violence, or more serious situations also lead to this situation.

Relationships are complex, and commitment, respect, and trust are fundamental factors. When these disappear or have never existed, it is very possible that there is no illusion of fighting for the relationship.

Thus, in certain circumstances it is important that to ensure your own happiness, you need to consider an alternative future. Relationships don't always have to be eternal. Now facing a separation can also be a challenge. Next we develop some ideas to be able to face it.

SIGNS THAT YOUR RELATIONSHIP IS OVER

Analyzing your relationship, the behavior, the mood of you and your significant other, can help make a decision. In some cases, just one problem is enough to determine the break. In other cases, the struggle to renew the relationship may be tougher.

It is positive to assess whether there are any of these indicators in the relationship. Several examples are

- Lack of communication or absence of sexual desire
- Lack of respect and commitment
- Lack of desire to spend time together, discussions
- Indifference to infidelity

If there is no love, commitment, passion, trust, and respect, it may be time to take action. Otherwise, you may fall into self-deception, and the only thing you will finally achieve is to extend the suffering and anxiety of both people.

12 POWERFUL AFFIRMATIONS TO ASSIST YOU THROUGH A DIVORCE

No matter the reason or who initiated the breakup, you will feel a sense of detachment and fear. A divorce can make your life change abruptly, and in most cases it is hard to get through the workday, stay productive, and be happy.

It may seem that you will never be happy and complete again. You can even question your self-worth. You might be thinking that you are not capable of raising your kids alone. There is so much uncertainty that you feel lost.

The good news is that things will get better. Believe me, you are actually evolving to become the best version of yourself. You have to trust me!

But one thing is true, and that is that in order to change your life, you must first change your thoughts.

You can take back control of your life. All you have to do is to be in charge of your thoughts, feelings, and decisions. You will start to heal when you start focusing on what you want.

HOW TO CALM YOUR JOURNEY

When you are going through a divorce, it is normal to feel anxiety and panic. Your brain will protect you by creating a fight response. This fight response can become harmful to your body when you experience it for a long time.

It is at this stage where you can get stuck in your mind and in your life in a pattern of negativity, and not even the biggest scissors can cut out the layer of protection you have created.

Right here, at this moment, you need to focus on creating a different and new response to deal with these feelings.

But for you to be capable of creating a new experience, first you need to change your mindset.

This means that you need to be aware of your negative thoughts and attitudes and learn how to let them go. Here are 12 affirmations that will help you through a divorce.

I UNDERSTAND WHY

HOW TO START CHANGING YOUR THOUGHTS

Before reading these powerful affirmations, it is important to take a few deep breaths. Mentally scan your body and determine if you are holding tension in any part. If you find that tension, it is time to breathe into it and let go.

Keep in mind that the best time to repeat these affirmations is before your mind attacks. So try to repeat them as soon as you wake up and then right before you go to sleep.

Affirmations right before you fall asleep are not only powerful, but they are the perfect way to end your day in a positive way.

These affirmations will speak to you in the "I" form as if you are leading yourself through the process.

You can repeat all of the affirmations below, or you can center your attention in just one that will be your guide throughout your day.

Remember these affirmations are just a few powerful words that will support your intention about how you want to live and how you want to be.

If you are ready, let's begin:

1. I am confident, strong, and energetic, and I am improving my life every day.
2. I am grateful for the lessons I learned in my past relationship.
3. I am a magnet for great and exciting things.
4. I love and accept myself.
5. I control my emotions and feelings with mindfulness.
6. I am a strong, brave woman who is raising two kids, maintaining a household, paying all the bills, and

working toward a more fulfilling career—and I am doing all of these things on my own!
7. I am in love with my life.
8. I forgive myself for getting divorced.
9. I am still the same beautiful and attractive woman I was when I first got married.
10. I am learning to trust again by first trusting myself, my own good judgment, and my gut instincts.
11. I am filled with an abundance of positivity and joy.
12. I am happy and hopeful.

Finally, remember that it is normal to feel sad, angry, and confused. Be confident that these feelings will lessen over time.

These powerful affirmations will create positive mental visions and will make you feel more optimistic. Saying these affirmations as soon as you wake up, before you go to sleep, and as often as possible throughout the day, your thoughts will change as you improve your self-esteem and avoid judgments of failure.

Just remember, "When the morning comes, let it go, this too shall pass."
OK Go.

7

Queen Sasha's Breakthrough

After that seven-letter word came out of Sasha's mouth, Terrance disappeared for two weeks.

Two weeks of not seeing or hearing from her husband.
Two weeks of Sasha calling Terrance non-stop.
Two weeks of unanswered phone calls.
Two weeks of unanswered voicemails.
Two weeks of paragraphs being texted with no reply.
Sasha left every bit of emotion in her texts and voicemails.
The messages ranged from anger to sorrow.
From "I'm strong and I don't need you"
To "Baby, I'm sorry. Come back home."

Sasha felt that she had lost control of her life, and she also felt that she had lost the life she always wanted for her and her daughters.

"Tiffany, I never felt so low… so desperate…

Even though Terrance wasn't returning my calls or texts, I knew he would come back home and we would be able to figure something out.

He eventually came home, but not to work things out or even to pack up his belongings.

He came home to put me out of the house.

He told me the kids would stay with him, and I had to go."

I UNDERSTAND WHY

Sasha went on to tell me that Terrance told her that he knew she couldn't afford to live in the home by herself without his portion of the rent. Sasha began to cry as she explained to me that somehow she had become financially dependent on him, and it left her in a place where she felt that she was at Terrance's mercy.

"Tiffany, I begged and cried for him to allow me to stay in the home and pay his portion, as I was taking care of his children and was still his wife.

He didn't care.

He told me that if I stayed, he would leave.

I left, but I took my babies with me.

The first night was tough. We stayed at a hotel, and I tried to make it seem like we were having a nice little girls' night.

Makayla had so many questions. I couldn't even answer half of them.

I eventually had to call my sister to ask if we could stay with her until I found a place for me and the children to live.

'Sasha, you allowed that man to put you out of your house?' asked my sister Tracy.

I could feel the judgment. I was always private when it came to my relationship and any issues that Terrance and I were dealing with.

Honestly I feel like my family partially blamed me because everyone loved Terrance. He had become their family.

We wound up staying with my sister for three weeks before I found an apartment much smaller than the house we were put out of. I felt horrible. Like I failed my babies.

But like my mother always says, 'Just because there is sorrow don't mean that there won't be a tomorrow, and the show must go on.'"

Sasha continued to tell me how the first month after moving out of the home was difficult, as she had to handle her job, trying to keep normalcy in her daughters' lives, and answering all questions that family and friends asked her without having a mental breakdown.

"Tiffany, it was too much for me. I wanted to check out. How wasn't this a dream… a nightmare… I just wanted my life to go back to what it was. I was even starting to think that Terrance cheating on me wasn't that bad, and I could have handled everything better.

I wanted things to get better, but as always, when it rains it pours.

A month and a half after separating from Terrance, I got a text message from him.

Terrance: *Hey Sasha … I need to see my girls*

I didn't respond right away because part of me wanted to say fuck off, but I knew my daughters missed him so much, and I didn't want to cause more pain in their lives.

Two days later I responded.

Sasha: *Ok, are you free Saturday I can drop them off*
Terrance: *Yea bring them to my house*

He was trying to get a reaction out of me, and I didn't have any more energy.

That Saturday came, I packed up Makayla and Ravyn and brought them over to Terrance's house.

When I rang the doorbell, a short, caramel-toned, very pregnant female opened the door.

I couldn't believe he moved his side chick into my house.

She smiled at me and then yelled, 'Babe, the kids are here.'"

Sasha then informed me that her first reaction was to cuss the side chick out and grab her kids and just go back home, but when

I UNDERSTAND WHY

she went to grab Ravyn's hand and tell Makayla to go back to the car, Terrance had already shown up at the door, and Makayla was already running in her father's direction.

"No matter how wrong the situation was, I didn't want the girls to suffer any more than what they had been through already."

Sasha then told me that she let the girls stay the weekend, and she went home and cried the entire time from sunup to sundown.

"Crying became my normal. Things were getting so bad my boss pulled me in to talk with me regarding my performance. I went from my boss recommending me for higher positions to warnings of possible write-ups. I was losing myself.

After two months, Terrance served me with divorce papers.

I thought paying for a lawyer was not an option. We didn't have anything worth fighting for other than the girls.

'I want full custody, Sasha.'

'Are you trying to take my babies from me?' You were barely home when we were a family. How the hell do you think you can take care of the kids on your own?'

'Jillian. She will be here.'

Click.

Was he serious? After all that I had already been through, Terrance thought that his mistress would be raising my children while I'm alive?! After that conversation I tapped into my savings and hired a lawyer. I realized a civil divorce was not going to happen.

It took six months for everything to be worked out in court/mediation.

The judge went with joint custody. Legal and physical. According to the judge, being that we live in the same town, joint custody wouldn't hurt the girls' school performance or make for many changes to take place… whatever that meant.

Having my children with me for only part of the week was difficult. I felt myself slipping into this deep depression, like I was a zombie just going through my day with no feelings.

I didn't think things would change until one day Makayla told me that she missed me even when she was around me.

That hurt and was the realist thing I'd heard from anyone.

Out of all the advice and pep talks that were given to me by friends and family, my daughter's words were what got me to realize I needed to change.

And so here we are."

After Sasha told me her story, we worked together on creating a weekly schedule on working through the steps needed for her transformation.

STEP 1

ACKNOWLEDGE: Like many other women, Sasha had to acknowledge the fact that her marriage was over. Even though Sasha and Terrance had been divorced for six months, Sasha still held on to the hope that Terrance would come back to her as the man she'd originally fallen in love with.

"I can't believe I'm going to tell you this, but sometimes I wear my wedding ring when I go to places that I know people don't know me," Sasha confessed.

"Do you know why you put on your wedding ring, Sasha?" I asked.

"Yes, it makes me feel at ease. That ring became part of who I am. It allows to me to forget all the pain that I endured and just go back to the life I once had."

Sasha went on to tell me about how beautiful the ring was and how it was an upgrade gift from Terrance on their fifth anniversary.

I UNDERSTAND WHY

According to Sasha, she didn't originally feel like wearing her ring was wrong until the day she ran into her sister's friend, and the friend congratulated her on her new engagement.

"I told her thank you, Tiffany. I was so shocked and caught off guard and embarrassed that all I could do was smile as she grabbed my hand and told me how beautiful the ring was.

Later on that week, my sister called me and asked why did her friend ask about an engagement."

Sasha paused and then went on to tell me that she always felt like she was in her sister's shadow and how her marriage to Terrance and his success was the proof that she wasn't just some silly girl who got knocked up in college.

For Sasha, her goal for the step of acknowledgement was to be honest with herself about being a divorced woman, which also meant no longer wearing her wedding ring on random occasions.

STEP 2

EMBRACE: After acknowledging how Sasha felt it was now time to embrace her feelings, She spoke about how she felt hurt and betrayed by Terrance. She discussed her feelings of being unworthy and feeling judged by her family. Every session we had during the embracing period, we discussed in detail how she felt and the assignments that had been given to her the week prior.

"I never thought I would say this, but the feeling I'm trying to understand and embrace is the feeling of relief," Sasha admitted. "Is that normal? Is it wrong?"

I told Sasha that there are no right or wrong feelings to have during this process. I explained to her that relief is actually normal and shows growth.

"I guess I am just relieved that I don't have to deal with the constant arguments and worrying about where and who he is with. I'm also relieved that my daughters are no longer witnessing the relationship that Terrance and I had. It was so toxic."

Sasha's sessions weren't always as upbeat. Sometimes they consisted of nothing but silent tears as she unpacked all her feelings, and we tried to sort through what these feelings meant to her. But eventually she was able to embrace all the feelings she'd been trying to avoid, and it was time to move to the third step. Acceptance.

STEP 3

ACCEPTANCE: For Sasha, acceptance did not come easily.

"Tiffany, I don't get what I have to accept," Sasha complained. "I know who I am."

"Great! Tell me," I encouraged.

Sasha sat silent then gave me a list of generic traits but nothing in-depth.

"Sasha, you have to know who you are in order to accept the woman that you have become. This step is where you find the positive in situations that you may not have been too happy about," I answered.

Over time, Sasha realized that she had to accept the fact that she was a single mother and enjoy the relationship she had with her children, accept that she was a woman who lost her way and was working toward getting back to a new and improved version of herself. She also had to accept the fact that she wasn't happy with the position she was working at her job and was willing to make sacrifices to put her in the position that she deserved.

"See, Sasha, you can not make changes to things you are not aware of. Awareness and acceptance are key. Being honest with yourself is important," I explained to her.

After Sasha worked on accepting the woman she currently was, she was able to move on to the fourth step.

STEP 4:

FORGIVENESS: During this step, I encouraged Sasha to make a list of anything in her life that made her angry or affected her in a way that she did not like.

Sasha's list consisted of her marriage and her strained relationship with her family.

"You know, Tiffany, it's not that I'm upset that we got a divorce. Because I feel like that was honestly for the best. I'm just upset that he lost respect for me and that I allowed him to be disrespectful for so long."

As Sasha worked through her feelings, she realized that there was a lot of anger she also held on to from past family drama.

Sasha shared with me that she always felt that she wasn't good enough when it came to her family. She explained that her parents didn't believe in having children out of wedlock, being divorced, and held the children to high expectations career-wise.

"My sister Tanya and I were always in some type of competition. We are four years apart, and I always felt that I lived in her shadow."

Sasha continued to tell me that Tanya was the child that her parents were most proud of.

"Tanya went to law school and married a doctor. Her wedding was beautiful, unlike mine and Terrance's. Terrance and I were young when we got married with already one child. Money was tight, so we had a small wedding because that's all we could afford," Sasha stated.

"You know, to this day my father still makes comments like I should have paid closer attention to Tanya, and my life wouldn't be the way it is now."

After Sasha was fully able to explain her family dynamic and how her divorce had affected her, she asked me, "So now what? Am I just supposed to forgive them?"

"If you want, but that's not the point of this step," I answered.

I went on to explain to Sasha that this step of forgiveness wasn't really about forgiving the people that wronged you or hurt you in your life; it's about truly dealing with any negativity in your life, forgiving yourself and replacing the space that held on to any hurt or ill feelings with peace, love, and happiness.

Too often in life, people hurt us and try to tear us down, and nine out of ten times, when that happens we fall into negative thinking patterns.

Our self-esteem starts to drop.

We begin doubting our talents and our strengths.

We begin to let ourselves down.

And that is why forgiveness is important. We have to forgive ourselves because at the end of the day we hold the power.

Self-love is empowering.

"Think about this," I said to Sasha. "How many times have you heard a woman talking about a bad decision she made in a relationship and then say how stupid she was? That woman needs to understand her situation, find healing and then needs to forgive herself."

Negative self-talk does not bring about healing.

I UNDERSTAND WHY

After Sasha was able to truly forgive herself, she then was able to set healthy boundaries and practice making sure she didn't take on any of the negativity that people tried to put on her.

STEP 5

LOVE YOURSELF—The Transformation

Sasha's goal for the rebuilding coaching was to have peace in her life, have pride in herself, and for her happiness not to be contingent on her marital/relationship status.

"All right, so we are finally at my favorite part of the healing process… I like to call this the transformation," I said to Sasha with a smile.

I had Sasha make a list of some short-term and long-term goals, and we worked together on planning how these goals would be achieved.

One of Sasha's main goals was to get her certs in HR and apply for an opening position at her job. At first she was slightly nervous and worried about how she would be able to juggle school and the girls, but Sasha made a decision that she had to invest in herself if she wanted to be in a better financial situation. It wasn't easy. Sasha told me about the long nights completing homework assignments, but over time she was able to get used to the late nights studying and keeping herself and her daughters on a tight schedule.

About two months after Sasha started the HR program, she received an email from her job stating that they were interested in hiring her for a higher position and much better pay.

"Tiffany, I can't believe I got the job. I mean, I knew the interview went well, but I can't believe it went that well," Sasha said excitedly.

"Well, I can. Congratulations, Sasha," I responded.

Over time, Sasha continued to work on herself and build the life that she was deserving of. She would update me on her relationship with her family and how she feels now that since she took back the power of her life, she no longer feels as though she is living to prove something to them.

Sasha even told me that her co-parenting with Terrance has been less hectic over the past few months and how she is no longer affected by his many women that he has in and out of the house as long as they show respect to Makayla and Ravyn.

"I never in my life thought that I would be okay with Terrance and his girlfriends, but here we are co-parenting and working on doing what's best for our daughters without wanting to strangle one another in the process. I feel like Terrance and I have definitely come a long way," Sasha told me during one of her sessions.

A couple weeks later Sasha gave me another update regarding Terrance.

"He wants to work on us," Sasha stated, starting her session without any other key information.

"I'm sorry, who are we talking about?" I asked, slightly confused.

"Terrance," she whispered.

"I see. What are your thoughts?" I asked.

Sasha went on to tell me that she wasn't expecting for Terrance to ever try and come back into her life romantically.

"I've been so caught up with working on me, I just haven't even thought about dating just yet and especially haven't thought about being with Terrance. I feel like that is going backwards," Sasha stated honestly. "Wait, what am I talking about? This is the same man that tried to take my daughters from me and kicked me out of my home, not to mention all the cheating… and he is with a whole new female."

Sasha and I went over her feelings and every truthful thought that had crossed her mind.

I then had Sasha complete a *what I bring to the table* activity.

Sasha made a list of all the things she brought to the table when it came to being in a relationship and also a list of some realistic non-negotiables in regard to what she wants from a man she is dating.

"Okay, so now are we going to fill in what he brings to the table?" Sasha asked me curiously.

"Nope," I responded. "My suggestion is for you to ask Terrance a specific question and let him tell you what he brings to the table so that you can have the information that you need to assist you in making your decision."

The next session, Sasha started the conversation telling me how she and Terrance met up to talk, and when he brought up his feelings and stated that he wanted his wife back, Sasha answered him with, "I understand why you would want me, but why would I want you?"

8

No Baby Mama Drama Over Here

5 SINGLE MOM SURVIVAL TIPS

"And so rock bottom became the solid foundation on which I rebuilt my life." - J.K. Rowling

Parenthood is challenging, especially if you are a single mom. For single moms, there are many stressful and lonely days. Unfortunately, there are more than 12 million single-parent families in the United States, and more than eighty percent of those are single-mom homes. The good news is that even though raising children can be tough, there are many single moms that are successful, and there are several ways to make the job easier. Here are five survival tips to stay organized to keep yourself sane and happy.

1. TAKE CONTROL OF YOUR FINANCES

One of the biggest concerns of single moms is money. The reality is that millions of single moms are trying to pay monthly bills. It is challenging to find a balance between work and family. However, taking control of your finances is vital as a single mother. There are three main things you must do to survive financially.

I UNDERSTAND WHY

Make a budget - There are two main things you must know as a single mother: your total income and total expenses. You need to add up your monthly income, and don't forget to include any income from a side job or part-time work. The next step is to add what you are spending each month. Include things like:

- Housing
- Utilities
- Cell phone
- Child care
- Transportation
- Groceries
- Insurance

Shop Wisely - It is essential to develop an attitude toward money. Make sure to:

- Check weekly ads
- Use coupons
- Take advantage of price matching policies
- Make a list when going to the grocery store
- Donate - Even though it might seem contradictory to donate a portion of your income, this is the perfect way of expressing trust in the Universe's faithfulness to meet your financial needs.

2. BECOMING BOTH MOM AND DAD

It is normal to worry about your kids being okay without a dad around the house. But the truth is that you can't be mom and dad; you are just one person. Trying to be both a mom and a dad only creates an impossible goal for you.

You have to accept that you are a single mom who is raising kids who don't have a dad in their daily life activities. The good news is that you don't have to cover the other person's job.

All you can do is control what you can by establishing priorities so your kids can grow up feeling confident. Stop feeling sorry for yourself, and create the life that you and your children need and deserve.

3. GET ORGANIZED

Make a priority to set up a system for your family to save time and to give your kids consistency.

It is essential to develop a daily routine and stick to it. You have to remember that kids like consistency. When you set a morning routine, everyone is ready to go, and there are no lunches or things forgotten at home accidentally.

Try to create a meal-time list, so you know what to buy at the grocery store. This could prevent chaos during a busy week.

4. DEALING WITH CO-PARENTING

Coping with co-parenting is challenging, and it can take some time for you to discover what is best for you and your family. Follow these basic guidelines when first adjusting to co-parenting.

- Do not talk bad about your ex in front of your children.
- Coordinate a shared calendar to make it easier to organize everything that is going on. Your kid will be grateful if you set a schedule to establish time with you and his or her father.

- Do not withhold your kids from their father. Be willing to accept reasonable alterations to the usual plan.

5. JOIN A SUPPORT GROUP

It is wiser to connect with other single moms with similar situations to provide you with the type of support that you need for your well-being. Look for single moms groups in your area to give and receive the encouragement and advice that could help you when you need it. Being a single mom can be lonely, and connecting with people who live close to you is a great way to cope with your new life successfully.

HOW TO TALK TO YOUR CHILDREN ABOUT THE BREAKUP

"Accept what is, let go of what was, and have faith in what will be."
Sonia Ricotti

Children do well with consistency. When they have dependable routines, they feel safe. It is important as a parent to tell your children of imminent changes.

When you and your partner decide to separate, you need a plan to tell your children. Children need to be told by their parents that they are separating. Remember, most children don't need to know the reasons why the separation happened.

You want to help your children get through the process as healthy and resilient as possible.

When you discuss with your children about separation, stay focused on the basic, objective facts. Do not focus on the past or the wrongdoing of either parent. Just explain in a simple calm way the arrangements for future parenting. Restore confidence by telling them how much both of you love them.

Just remember that the more you expose your children to conflict, the worse it is for them. Don't involve them in the negative details of your relationship, as this will affect your relationship with them and with their other parent. Your goal should be to affect them as little as possible.

For children to function well, they need to have less exposure to conflict and the details of their parents' relationship breakdown.

TIPS FOR TALKING TO CHILDREN ABOUT YOUR SEPARATION

1. TELL YOUR CHILDREN AS SOON AS POSSIBLE

You have to remember that children are exceptionally insightful, and they know that something is going on. So don't keep it a secret; the sooner they know, the less they will worry.

But don't make the mistake of telling them if you and your partner are only considering a separation. Wait until you know for sure.

It is important to find a moment where you have plenty of time afterward to stay near your children. Remember, they need to feel supported and loved, so don't do it in a rush.

Even if your partner and you are not speaking to each other, try to agree on what to tell your children and do it together. This way you will avoid confusion, as it will demonstrate that it was a mutual decision.

But if this is not possible because you can't exchange two words without fighting, don't force it. It is better to have separate calm conversations than to fight in front of your children, as this will be a disaster.

Keep the discussion simple and answer all their questions. Children want to know how their life will be impacted, so be sympathetic, tender, and prepared with solid answers.

2. DON'T LIE

Don't lie to your children by saying something like *We are going to try living apart for a while.* It is cruel and unnecessary to give them a reason to hope you will get back together.

It is better to tell them the truth. This way they can grieve, accept, and adjust to their new reality.

Even if you are hopeful that this could be something temporary, don't tell them. If you reconcile it will be a great surprise; if not, they will not be disappointed again.

3. DON'T HIDE YOUR FEELINGS

Remember, ending a relationship is sad, and it is okay to have a sad conversation. Don't try to be stoic. Don't worry if you end up crying when you tell your kids about the breakup. It is normal. When you hide your feelings it creates more confusion.

4. DON'T ASK YOUR CHILDREN TO CHOOSE

Avoid involving your children in the decision related to the separation. Don't put them into the distressing position of having to choose sides. You have to keep in mind that this is not a contest, and it is harmful to your children. You as parents need to make decisions based on your kids' best interests.

Finally, avoid putting pressure on yourself to do it perfectly. Most children will not remember the words, but they will remember how you make them feel.

Yes, practice what you are going to say and anticipate likely questions, but keep in mind that you can't predict their reactions.

It doesn't have to be perfect; it just needs to make your kids feel safe and loved.

HOW TO COPE WITH YOUR EX DATING AGAIN

"When it hurts to move on, just remember the pain you felt hanging on."
Anonymous

Seeing your ex for the first time with another partner is hard. Why? Because most of us feel expendable, rejected, and out of control.

Every therapist will tell you to put this person in your past and move on. But the truth is that it is easier said than done. You should use healthy ways to process the news.

I UNDERSTAND WHY

First, it is important to set strong limits between yourself and your ex. This is the time that you need to pay attention to your needs and help yourself move forward.

Here are some tips on how to move on.

1. DON'T FOLLOW YOUR EX ON SOCIAL MEDIA

When you keep following your ex on social media, you will start comparing yourself with his/her new partner. Remember, you need to focus on you!

Avoid the temptation to ask mutual friends about your ex's new relationship. Believe me, you will feel devastated.

When you compare yourself with others, it often makes you unhappy, even if you have enough and should be happy with what you have.

If you start to compare yourself, stop it! And then start thinking about all the things you do have, the blessings in your life, and the people you have. You will notice how you will start feeling happier with your life.

2. AVOID NEGATIVE SELF-TALK

Negative self-talk is something that you usually experience when you find out your ex is dating someone else. It is common to say to yourself: *"I am such an idiot for still caring."*

When you talk to yourself this way, you are creating stress and unhappiness. Instead, try to use positive self-talk. When you acknowledge that you are not an idiot for still caring, but a loving and generous person, you will feel better. Remember, to still love or care about a person who was part of your life is okay.

3. REMIND YOURSELF WHY YOU BROKE UP

Even if you are feeling sad that your ex is dating again, there should be a reason why you are not together anymore. Remember all the reasons why your relationship didn't work out.

Write down all his/her bad behaviors and annoying habits and read them. Thinking about this will help you realize that it was for the best to end things.

Remember, it is okay to feel hurt, upset, or angry by a breakup that caught you off-guard.

4. BE PATIENT

As I mentioned before, dealing with your ex dating again can make you feel depressed and hurt because you didn't expect him/her to do it so soon. You have to understand that people heal at different times and rates.

The best thing you can do is to take care of yourself and wait until you feel it is the right time to find a new, healthy relationship.

Now is the perfect time to date with your friends. Your friends will fulfill your days in ways that a love-partner never could. Go traveling, to lunch dates, or just sit on the couch and talk. You will be amazed at how much better you will feel. Good friends are unconditional, reciprocal, and capable of healing your broken heart.

I UNDERSTAND WHY

5. DON'T TALK BAD ABOUT YOUR EX

Don't spend time talking bad about your ex to make yourself feel better. Every time you do this, you are preventing yourself from moving forward.

Avoid turning all conversations around your ex. You should be thinking about you and your feelings.

BOTTOM LINE

Getting over the fact that your ex is dating someone else is not the easiest thing to do. You have to remember that this could be a major blow to your self-esteem and mental health.

The best thing you can do is to stop comparing yourself with other people. Focus on you and don't forget to develop a positive mindset. Give yourself time to heal and move on at your pace.

Finally, remember that all the pain you are suffering right now will create a better version of you. Use your feelings to motivate you to do new things. You are, after all, living your best life!

CO-PARENTING ADVICE

"This is probably one of the most difficult challenges any parent could face—learning to love the other parent enough to make the children first."
Iyanla Vanzant

Co-parenting is challenging. It is key to find a way to make joint custody work so your kids can have stability, security, and a close relationship with both parents. Joint custody settlements can be exhausting, especially if you have a problematic relationship with your ex-partner.

It is common to feel worried about your ex's parenting skills or to think that you will never be able to overcome all the problems in your relationship. But having both parents involved in their kids' lives is the best way to protect their needs.

It is essential to notice that the quality of the relationship between parents has a strong influence on the children's mental and emotional well-being. The good news is that it is possible to co-parent successfully with your ex.

Here are some great tips to remain calm and make joint custody work for you and your kids.

1. SEPARATE YOUR FEELINGS

As a parent, you need to separate your feelings from what is best for your kids. You have to remember that co-parenting is not about you, but your child's security, confidence, and happiness.

Never put your child in the middle. Keep in mind that your resentment or bitterness about your separation are your issues, not your kids'. Keep unresolved problems with your ex away from your children.

Your primary goal should be to keep your child out of your relationship problems. If you have something to say to your ex, never use your kids as the messenger. It is best to call or email directly.

It is vital never to make them feel that they have to choose between you and your ex. Your children have the right to have both parents in their lives.

I UNDERSTAND WHY

2. HEAL YOURSELF

It is essential to healing yourself to be able to move on from the past. When parents are still angry with each other, even the smallest decision is a problem. You need to be able to self-reflect and think about the relationship as a completed one instead of a failed one. When you are happier, it is easier to co-parent effectively.

3. MAKE CO-PARENTING AN OPEN DIALOGUE WITH YOUR EX

It is crucial to make co-parenting an open dialogue with your ex through email, texting, or face-to-face conversations. If this is not possible now, there are websites where you can upload schedules to share information, so you and your ex don't have to communicate directly.

Here are some methods you can use to improve communication with your ex.

- Speak to your ex as a business partner.
- Avoid demands. Instead, try to make requests.
- Try not to overreact.
- Commit to communicate regularly to discuss your kids' issues.
- Always keep the conversations kid-focused.

Practice quick stress relief techniques such as:

- Breath focus
- Meditation
- Yoga
- Repetitive prayer

4. REMAIN CONSISTENT

It would be best if you remained as a team so your kids can live under the same basic set of norms at each home. If there is no consistency between your home and your ex's, your children will get confused.

Even though the rules don't have to be the same between both houses, you need to establish consistent guidelines. Important rules such as homework issues, curfews, and prohibited activities should be the same in both houses. It is wiser to follow similar consequences for breaking the rules also.

Try your best to have a consistent schedule, meals, homework, and bedtime so your kids can adjust better to their new lifestyle.

5. DO NOT TREAT YOUR KID AS A FRIEND

Sometimes you can make the mistake of treating your children as a friend and discuss adult topics like money and parenting with them. Your children should not be involved in adult decisions.

Giving kids too much power to decide what they want to do can lead to poor choices and diminish respect for a parent. This could lead to your child feeling guilty, depressed, or anxious.

I UNDERSTAND WHY

SINGLE MOM SUPPORT GROUPS

"Anything is possible when you have the right people there to support you."
Misty Copeland

It is challenging for single mothers to balance it all from making enough money to make ends meet to discipline and entertainment. The truth is that it can be hard to find someone who relates to your situation. You want a group where you can talk about things and be heard.

Single parents have to deal with stress, anxiety, exhaustion, depression, and feelings of isolation. Besides, you want to find the right models to offer positive influences on the kids as they grow up.

Single mom support groups are a great place to find people that truly can relate to your situation. So how do you find the right group? To help you evaluate your options, here are some things you must look at before you join one.

1. HOW MANY TIMES THE SUPPORT GROUP MEETS

Before you join a single parent support group, it is important to know when and where they meet. Some groups only meet bi-weekly or once per month; if you need ongoing support, look for one that meets weekly. A good option is single mom support groups that combine face-to-face meetings with online discussion boards.

2. HOW MUCH IT COSTS

Usually, you will need to pay a fee to be part of a single parent support group. Make sure to find out how much you will have to pay to know if you can afford it. Some single mom support groups offer additional benefits for their members, so make sure to know how much it costs to see if it is worth the investment.

3. CAN I BRING MY CHILDREN

Make sure to find a single parent support group that offers childcare during their meetings. You should ask if this feature has an additional cost or if members volunteer in the childcare room from time to time. If childcare is offered, it is essential to know what type of activities are available for children. Remember, joining a single parent support group allows your children to spend time with peers who are going through a similar situation. Keep in mind that some support groups provide counseling for older children and therapy activities for younger kids.

4. IS THE GROUP OPEN TO EVERYONE

Generally, single parent support groups are open to both single moms and dads, but it is always wiser to ask if there are any limitations. For instance, maybe the group is only available for single parents raising school-age children. Knowing if the group has any particular interest is key to finding the best fit for you and your family. If your biggest concern is to receive emotional support, look for a group that offers mentorship or coaching. On the other hand, if you need help with your financial situation, look for a group that focuses on giving economic workshops.

5. IS THE GROUP ANONYMOUS

It is essential to determine if the group is anonymous or not, especially if they offer online boards. For instance, single parent support groups that offer a Facebook group to have constant connections with other members are usually not anonymous. Yes, they can be a closed group, but anyone can screenshot your posts, so be careful not to post anything sensitive on social media. Social media can provide proof in family courts. It is better to find a single parent support group that offers a forum where you can post anonymously if you are going through a tough divorce. Here are some online single parents groups you might not know about:

- Beanstalk Anonymous Single Mother Forum
- National Council for Single Mothers and their Children
- Single Mum Vine

Finally, if you can't find a single parent support group in your area, you can always consider starting your own. You can become the founding member and develop a support group that meets your needs.

You can begin by making a list of all the single parents you know. Once you have the list, start by contacting each person individually and ask if they would like to participate in a newly single parent support group you are starting. Don't get discouraged if there are not many parents at your first meeting; the group will grow with time.

HOW TO DATE WHEN YOU HAVE CHILDREN

"If you're brave enough to say goodbye, life will reward you with a new hello."
Paulo Coelho

Starting to date again as a single parent can seem intimidating. It is difficult to know where to start looking or how you find the time to go out, or even worse, how much and when to tell your kids.

ARE YOU READY TO START DATING?

It is important to understand that every person is unique and moves at different times and rates, so there is no *"right"* time to start dating. It could be six months post-divorce or ten years.

Better questions are:

- Why do you want to start dating?
- What are you looking for in a partner?
- What voids are you looking to fill?

For instance, if you want to start dating because you want to get out of the house, it is a better idea to call a friend. Keep in mind that if you are expecting to fulfill your needs by dating, you are not ready to start again.

I UNDERSTAND WHY

Single parents should work on themselves first to know what they want and need.

TIME FOR DATING

One common problem with single parents is that they don't have the time to start dating. And, unfortunately, this is true. Finding time for yourself is key. It is important to spend time with friends without kids and time alone.

If your schedule is too busy, you might want to rethink dating. But if you want to date you will need to make time in your life for it. Find people that can help and support you. For instance, if you are co-parenting, you can use the days without kids to date.

If you are alone, you can use sites such as MomMeetMom.com where you can find other mothers in your area that could lead to a potential friend that might be able to babysit.

HOW TO MEET PEOPLE

Dating as a single parent isn't the same as when you were younger. It is not wise to pick up dates at bars if you are looking for a serious relationship.

The good news is that you can meet people in places such as your gym or your favorite coffee shop. Chances are you can meet another single parent at your kids' soccer matches or while you are waiting to pick them up after school.

The truth is once you decide that you want to start dating again and you send that message to the universe, you will find opportunities all around you. When you start recognizing these opportunities, you will notice how more receptive people are with you.

If meeting people in your regular activities seems hard, you can look into the internet dating scene. They are fun and flirty and perfect for those who are shy or busy, as you can get used to the idea of looking for love without the pressure.

Just be careful to always weigh the risks and benefits. Don't let fear make you pass up a good opportunity, but think a lot before deciding if it is right.

TALK TO YOUR KIDS

Finally, when you start dating as a single parent, it is not just about finding the time to go out. It is how your children will cope with your dating. Every kid is different, so be prepared for their reaction. For instance, your older kid may feel as if you are slipping away, while your younger one will quickly accept the idea and welcome a new person into their lives.

So before you begin dating again, you first need to talk to your kids. Once your kids know what is going on, it will be easier to find time to start dating again. You will look for ways to have extra time without hiding it or upsetting your kids.

Don't make the mistake to introduce them to every person you date, but you should not hide if you are dating either. Use your best judgment to decide how many details to share with them.

No matter how much you decide to tell your children, just don't lie to them. When you lie to them, you are creating trust issues down the road. Remember, the last thing you want is to cause a problem between you and your kids.

9

A Breakup to Queen Up Story
Queen Michelle's Story

Have you ever dated someone without a purpose? I mean just date just because, no real end goal in mind? Well, that's where Michelle was when she first met Derrick.

"I was at a point in my life where I was on dating sites trying to find someone to keep me from feeling lonely."

MEET MICHELLE

Michelle and her ex-boyfriend/current buddy with benefits, Derrick, were together for three years. I met Michelle a few months after her breakup with Derrick, and at this time they had transitioned into friends with benefits only. Michelle was in stage denial. Michelle told me she didn't understand how and why he had broken up with her. At this time, Michelle was still making attempts to get back with her ex but was very unsuccessful.

"I need someone to talk to.

I honestly can't get this man off my mind.

I go to bed just to end up dreaming of him and I wake up just to daydream about him.

I UNDERSTAND WHY

I met Derrick on a social media app.

I can't say that I was looking for anything serious, but I was looking for some light entertainment.

When Derrick first hit me up on the app he was smooth with it. And when we finally met up for our first date, we just clicked.

I was just getting out of a five-year relationship, and I was ready for a new experience.

Derrick was also recovering from a broken heart, and we both just wanted to erase the pain.

What's the saying? Easiest way to get over someone old is to get under someone new?!

And that was my plan—I just hated being by myself, and it's hard adjusting from being with someone for five years to now moving solo. I hated it.

My previous relationship was HOORRIIBBLLLEEEEE. I mean, Kevin and I dated for five years, and I was heartbroken when he dumped me. I tried being single but it didn't work, and I knew for certain I didn't want to be alone on my upcoming birthday, so I hopped on a dating site and tried to find someone that I could hang out with to keep my mind off of things.

And that's when I met Derrick.

Derrick's profile read: 'I'm a leader not a follower. Strong Black man who is looking for a queen. I believe the man is the head and the female is the neck ... The female's role is important because without the neck the head can't function properly.'

I thought that was different, and after Kevin I just wanted someone who had some common sense. Kevin had no goals, I felt a man that is claiming to be a leader must have some type of drive in his life, so I swiped right.

After I swiped right, I sent a message:

Shelly26: Every man is looking for a queen but do you know how to be a king?
Rick: Hi, yes I know how to lead, I know how to listen, I know how to compromise, and I definitely know how to provide…
Shelly26: Sounds good
Rick: Well I can show you better than I can tell you
Shelly26: Easy king… I don't know you like that
Rick: So let's get to know each other- I'm Derrick
Shelly26: I'm Michelle

Derrick and I wrote each other on the dating site for a few weeks, and I finally gave in and met up with him three days before my birthday.

Our first date was easygoing. We shared our past relationship stories and laughed over everything. I told him that my birthday was in three days, and he was determined to be my birthday date and would not take no for an answer.

Derrick and I became inseparable right away.

Truthfully now that I look back on things I don't know what it was about Derrick that reeled me in so strongly. Don't get me wrong; he's fine and the sex is a1… but I just always felt that I was following, and I don't mean following in the context of the Bible, but just what he said went. We spent time doing all the things that he loved and enjoyed, and initially I was fine with it, but over time I started to realize I didn't really have anything of my own.

Michelle went on to tell me about how her relationship with Derrick was. She described their relationship as two good people who made good partners. Derrick and Michelle dated for a few years, and they barely had any issues. According to Michelle, she felt they would make a good match because unlike her previous relationship, Michelle and Derrick didn't get into constant arguments, and Derrick seemed pretty easygoing.

"You know, Tiffany, I just felt secure with him. Derrick managed his money right, wasn't into the party scene, and definitely didn't do drama.

We were different, but over time I thought he was the one because of how simple we were.

We both were employed, believed in God, and didn't believe that yelling was effective communication.

Derrick was passionate about his line of work, and I loved that.

He worked as a manager at a bank and had big dreams to invest in real estate, and I believed in him.

At night we would listen to all the real estate podcasts or Audible books that pertained to investment.

He inspired me to look into myself and pursue my passion of starting a business. At first I had no clue as to what I was interested in, and then I decided to get a coach to help me narrow down my options and figure out what direction I truly wanted to start a business in. I decided to go with opening a dance studio.

When I was younger, dancing was everything that I loved. I never thought I was going to be some award-winning dancer, but it gave me a sense of peace and joy. So I decided why not go back to what puts a smile on my face in the first place?

But first I decided maybe I should freshen up on my dancing skills. So I began taking dance classes after work. And that's when the problems started.

'Hey, babe, I'm just finishing up playing ball with the boys. What's for dinner?' asked Derrick cheerfully.

'Dinner? Babe, I told you I had my dance class tonight. Remember?'

'Oh yeah… I forgot,' answered Derrick. 'What are you going to cook when you get home? I'm starving.'

'Babe, I told you tonight's class was pushed back to 8 and won't end till 10. I'm going to be too tired to cook when I get home later.'

'Shell, don't you just want to stay home and relax with me? Let's order in. Besides, we have to go to my event tomorrow morning and I want you to be at your best because I need you.'

'Uggh.' Michelle let out a slight agitated sigh before answering. 'Okay, I'll stay home tonight, but only this one time. You know it's important for me to continue to go to these classes.'

'Yeah, I know,' Derrick answered."

Michelle went on to tell me that that was her first of many missed dancing classes due to her having to cater to Derrick.

"Tiff, I tried everything to accommodate him so that my goals weren't interfering with the relationship. I would make dinner in advance so all he had to do was heat up his plate. He legit found issues with everything.

There was one night when we both had events to go at the same time. I thought it would have been easy as we just wouldn't be able to support each other for this one time because our schedules clashed. Nope! Derrick wasn't having it. He made it the biggest deal, and I couldn't understand why.

'Yo, so you really not coming with me to my real estate function tonight?' asked Derrick, who appeared annoyed.

'Derrick, I have a meeting tonight with Angie, and she said there are going to be some investors there so this is my chance to shoot my shot at opening up my dance studio.'

'Yeah, I get that, but this event is big to me as well. I get to pitch my ideas to the people that can make it happen… I don't get why you don't see how important this is to me.'

I UNDERSTAND WHY

'Naww, that's not fair, Derrick. Tonight is important for the both of us.'

'Shell, they don't know you. You are still trying to get your foot in the door, when I already got a seat at the table. My event is extremely important for us, and our future. Don't you care about building our future together?'

'You know I do," I answered.

'Then you understand how important it is for you to be there to support me! I'm not understanding how can we be a united front if you are over there trying to do your own thing? I need you, Shells. You have always been in my corner, and I need you there especially for tonight.'

I fell for it, Tiffany, over and over again I fell for every explanation he had to why I had to put my goal on the back burner. I wanted to build with him, but I started to feel like I was suffocating.

It didn't take much time for me to altogether 86 my idea of opening a dance studio, and I eventually stopped going to dance class. I love Derrick, but if there is one thing I regret, it would be giving up on something that brought me happiness. But unfortunately I didn't see my choice to put my goals on the backend that way at that time. I truly thought I was making the right decision by choosing to support my man.

Over time, Derrick eventually let go of the idea of investing in real estate when he wasn't getting the feedback he thought he should be getting. My relationship with Derrick was going fine, we just returned to our regular routine, but there was something I felt was missing. So I decided to go back to dance class because of the feeling of peace it gave me. To be honest, I wasn't sure how Derrick would feel about me going back to dance class because he still engaged in playing basketball with his boys daily. But of course, I was wrong. He cared. He complained about it. And he even went as far as saying if he couldn't get his business off the ground how would I be able to get mine? That shit hurt. It hurt because I realized that in this relationship all I would be able to do is follow."

  Michelle went on to explain to me the continuous ups and downs of her relationship with Derrick and the constant back and forth tug of war that took place every time Michelle gave her goals any attention. She also shared the good times, which is where she and Derrick were before he broke up with her.

  "I still can't believe we aren't together. I swear it makes no sense to me. We were good. I thought we were making strides to becoming stronger as a couple. Hell, we were even talking about marriage. The only thing I can think about that could have thrown us off track is the last disagreement we had two weeks prior to him packing up his stuff and moving out of the apartment. It wasn't even a big deal, but he made it into one."

  "Michelle, Michelle," yelled Derrick from the living room into a bedroom.

  "Yes, babe?"

  "What are you doing back there? I thought we were going to have movie night tonight."

  "We are. I just wanted to work on this last idea I had."

  "The movie starts at 9:10, and it's 8:30. I don't want to be late."

  "Okay, I'm coming!! You know one day, babe, we won't have to leave the house to go to the movies. We are going to have our own private theater in the basement!"

  "Oh yeah, babe?" asked Derrick, amused.

  "Yup, we will be living large off of the dance studio's income. You know my plan is to have a franchise."

I UNDERSTAND WHY

"Here you go again with this shit. I'm not living off of no woman's income," answered Derrick agitatedly.

"We can build together, babe."

"Michelle, can we not tonight? I just want to relax and have a good night," stated Derrick, annoyed.

"Yup.. me too," answered Michelle.

"After that conversation, the rest of the night was quiet. I was bothered by the lack of support I was receiving from Derrick, especially since I was nothing but supportive of him every step of his journey in everything that he does. I was getting closer to my goal of setting up my first studio, and I just didn't understand why he couldn't support me and be there for me like I was for him.

I remember that night before I went to bed I prayed, *Father God, if he isn't for me, please remove him from my life.* I'm not even sure what made me say that prayer. I loved Derrick, I still love Derrick. But what I do know is two weeks later I came home to an empty apartment. No furniture.

No Derrick.

No letter.

No hint.

No sign.

Just gone.

I messed up a good relationship with a great man all for some silly dream of opening up a dance studio.

I want him back…"

Drowning

I'm drowning in all my thoughts
Thoughts of you

TIFFANY SMITH

Thoughts of us

I'm screaming out for help
But it's like you don't see me
I'm trying
Desperately to get your attention
I'm sinking
With no one to rescue me

Will this be the end of me
Will I lose sight of what God has planned for me
Will I cower
Or will I stand tall
I dare not let this be the end of me

You gave me peace
Lies
You gave me happiness
Sometimes

You leave me to fend for myself
Grasping for the air to save me
'Cause ain't no one around me
I suffer
Suffocating from my tears and my screams
Gasping for air to revive me
Ima endangered species

10

How to Deal with the Pain of a Breakup

Whether you want the breakup or not, you still go through a mad one. When, however, you find that you hurt more than you thought possible, you will be able to manage the breakdown, you aren't on your own. Most of us are able to share the pain you feel right now. It's important to look over pain and find a way to live, even when the things look very bad when coping with the breakdown of ties.

It feels like pain never will end sometimes. It might even feel so daunting that you're struggling to deal with them, but pause and remember how many people deal with and succeed in their lives. You, too, will have the chance, if you are willing to deal in the right and healthy way, to conquer the pain of a broken heart.

So why is it so difficult to break down the pain? Maybe it's because it feels as if you're the only one with the pain you've suffered. It seems that people are in couples everywhere you look, while you're alone and miserable. Thinking endlessly about pain won't help you recover again, so you should work on improving and moving forward—I know it's easier said than done, yet it's possible. It will allow you to make better use of your resources and move on to the next chapter of your life. There are millions of men out there who are better than your husband.

Take the time to reconnect with friends you've missed from the moment you started dating. They will have their own breakdown stories and take your mind away from yours. Yet seek to be with uplifting friends instead of those who indulge in the struggles of life. You have to focus on all the great things you have to do for yourself, and your friends will support you. They care and want you to be happy and be frank about how you feel and how they can help you.

The first days after a breakup are the days you should mourn the ending of your relationship. But then it's time to get back to the swing of things by continuing to grow. You can't stand, and nothing remains still. It causes pain when faced with a breakup. Yet we plan for our future growth through this pain. Upload and don't hide what's difficult. Be not afraid of uncertainty, crises, or pain, as they are the causes for growth and change.

Life comes after a breakup, and it's up to you to take your hands and pick it up.

HOW TO KNOW WHEN TO LEAVE A MARRIAGE

Making the choice to leave my marriage was difficult. I felt overwhelmed with so many different emotions, from *Yeah this is the right decision* to *What the fuck am I going to do next?* even to *Damn, how can I live without him?*

Out of all the thoughts going through my mind the one that really had me unsure was, *Tiff, are you sure you're making the right choice?*

> "*Trust your instincts, and make judgments on what your heart tells you. The heart will not betray you.*"
> David Gemmell, Fall of Kings

Ending your marriage is one of the toughest decisions you are going to make in your life. Many people take a long time before making a firm decision about whether to stay or go.

There is no secret formula for knowing when is the right time to leave a relationship, and it can be stressful and confusing trying to decide.

It is hard to determine whether you are going through a tough time or if it is something more serious. The worst thing about it is that you think that leaving your marriage would mean you are a failure. This is especially true when there are children involved, as you don't want to let them down.

You need to understand that no one should be expected to remain in an unhappy marriage. You are not a failure; you are a strong person for choosing you. Remember, a lot of good can come from ending a marriage.

It is easy to forget that staying in an unhappy marriage can have long-term effects on your mental and emotional health. The truth is that people feel sad and grieve when they decide to end a marriage, but people who divorce do recover emotionally, and most find new and healthy ways to move on and be happy.

If you are thinking about leaving your marriage, here are six signs that can help you decide.

I UNDERSTAND WHY

6 SIGNS TO KNOW IF IT IS TIME TO END YOUR MARRIAGE

"Success is not final, failure is not fatal: it is the courage to continue that counts."
Winston Churchill

1. LACK OF PHYSICAL AFFECTION

Not having sex anymore is a warning sign. You need to keep in mind that it is the intimacy that differentiates a romantic relationship from other relationships you might have.

The lack of physical affection like kissing and hugging is a big red flag that you may have a real problem.

2. YOU THINK YOUR LIFE WILL BE BETTER WITHOUT YOUR SPOUSE

If you spend a lot of time daydreaming about how much better your life will be without your spouse, it is time to seek help.

Talk with your partner about why you are feeling this way. It is only fair that your spouse knows what is going on in the marriage, especially if you have children. Maybe a marital therapist can give both of you a second chance.

3. YOU ARE NOT IGNORING YOUR GUT

When things don't feel right they probably aren't. So listen to your gut! Remember, when your intuition talks, it is worth listening to. Your gut has the power to tell you what you do and do not want.

4. YOU DON'T TALK ANYMORE

If you are not having meaningful conversations besides what things need to get done, that is a warning sign that your relationship is having problems. When something happens in your life and you don't want to share it with your partner, this may be a sign that you prefer to share your needs outside the relationship.

5. THE BAD OUTWEIGHS THE GOOD

Every couple has problems, but when you don't seek solutions, suddenly the bad will outweigh the good. Marriages can become a vicious cycle of one problem after another. If you and your spouse don't seek help, you will end up with unsolvable issues.

6. YOU ARE CONTEMPLATING HAVING AN AFFAIR

When you are not happy with your spouse, you may be considering having an affair, either emotional, physical, or both. And thanks to technology, it is easier.

Remember, if your marriage is on the rocks, having an affair will only make things worse.

BOTTOM LINE

The best way to decide if you want to leave your marriage is to take a step back to see things more objectively. Never make any decisions if you are feeling confused or upset. You don't want to do something that you might regret later.

Try to answer these questions: Have the problems developed recently or has it been going on for a long time? Have you and your spouse sought help? If you decide to stay, are you doing it because you love your spouse or because you are afraid to be alone?

Finally, whatever you do decide, you have to keep in mind that the decision is one you and your partner should make. And stop worrying about what other people think or what you think you are supposed to do.

Remember you are a strong person capable of deciding what's best for you!

HOW TO ALLOW YOURSELF TO GRIEVE AFTER THE LOSS OF A RELATIONSHIP

Grief is a natural reaction to loss, and the breakup or divorce of a love relationship involves multiple losses:

- Loss of fellowship and sharing experiences (which may or may not have been consistently pleasurable)
- Loss of support, whether financial, intellectual, social, or emotional

- Loss of hope, plans, and dreams (which can be even more painful than practical losses)

Allowing yourself to feel the pain of these losses can be scary. You may fear that your emotions are too intense to bear, or that you will be trapped in a dark place forever. Just remember that grief is essential for the healing process. The pain of grief is precisely what helps you to leave the old relationship and move on. And no matter how strong your pain is, it won't last forever.

Tips to grieve after a breakup or divorce:

Do not fight your feelings - It is normal to have many ups and downs and feel many conflicting emotions, such as anger, resentment, sadness, relief, fear, and confusion. It is important to identify and recognize these feelings. While these emotions will often be painful, trying to repress or ignore them will only prolong the grieving process.

Talk about how you feel - Even if it is difficult for you to discuss your feelings with other people, it is very important to find a way to do it when you are distressed. Knowing that others are aware of your feelings will make you feel less alone with your pain and will help you heal. Writing in a diary can also be a useful outlet for your feelings.

Remember that moving forward is the ultimate goal - Expressing your feelings will free you in some way, but it is important not to stop at negative feelings or to analyze the situation too much. Getting caught in hurtful feelings like guilt, anger, and resentment will steal valuable energy and prevent you from recovering and moving on.

Remember that you still have a future - When you commit to another person, you create high hopes and dreams for a life together. After a breakup, it is difficult to let go of these aspirations. While lamenting the loss of the future you once imagined, rejoice in the fact that new hopes and dreams will eventually replace the old ones.

Know the difference between a normal reaction to a breakup and depression - The pain can be paralyzing after a break, but after a while, the sadness begins to disappear. Day by day, and little by little, you start moving forward. However, if you don't feel any momentum forward, you may be suffering from depression, and it may be time to talk with a professional. There is no shame in seeking out a therapist after a breakup/divorce. You need to make sure you are at your best so that you can get back on the grind and shine bright like a diamond. Because you know pressure makes diamonds. Difficult times make us strong. So go ahead and embrace that pain and turn it into a gain.

SELF-LOVE AFTER SEPARATION

When a relationship ends, it is common for us to feel the effect on our self-esteem.

The breakup of love usually occurs after an event that overflows previous unresolved and accumulated conflicts; rarely is it the result of a single isolated situation. It is understood that there were a series of circumstances that slowly cracked the bond until it was broken. Some say it's a reaction caused by both parties to a greater or lesser extent, lacking willingness, decision, control, communication, or a strategy to heal it.

However, due to intense emotions, it is usual for them to engage in the search for culprits. One or both can react aggressively, refusing to accept shared responsibility, placing themselves in the victim's place, and lashing out at the other, blaming them for everything with the intention of injuring their self-esteem by signaling that they have to be evaluated negatively.

Others decide to assume the guilt of separation, which causes or fuels thoughts of failure, inadequacy, and self-disqualification, considering that they could have done something better, that they failed again in love, or that they are not fit to love.

Those who suffer from emotional dependence and consider that they are being abandoned because they are insufficient or undesirable fall into a deep depression and completely bend their will before their loved one to try to keep their company. People who lived a super romantic love or an obsessive love are more prone to this. Few couples manage to separate in a calm way, with the interest of guaranteeing the well-being of the two individuals, understanding that the relationship was another experience in their lives, thanking the lessons they have left, forgiving the offenses received, and accepting responsibility for the wounds caused.

RECOVER YOUR SELF-LOVE AND MOVE ON

The termination of a sentimental relationship is not the end of your life or that of your ex-partner; it is a change and therefore a new beginning for both.

Don't waste your energy on looking for guilt; focus on healing, forgiving and growing. There were reasons to love him, so don't hate him now. Let him go.

I UNDERSTAND WHY

Do not despise what you had or punish yourself because it is over. Understand that there were things that contributed to your well-being and others that undermined it. Accept and learn.

Thanks to everything that happened in your relationship, you can learn about yourself, sentimental ties, and life in general. The gain of learning prevents you from thinking that you have been left empty-handed and surrender to frustration.

You are not a victim; you are a brave person who can overcome this current penalty. Make a list of all your strengths and abilities. No matter if some seem insignificant, all your qualities are important and useful.

A nail does not necessarily take out another nail; it can sink it further. Give yourself time to put everything in order, your feelings, thoughts, goals, habits and priorities.

If you constantly think of your ex, occupy your mind in other matters and try to do various activities. Perhaps you deprived yourself of some beneficial things for yourself—now is the time to do them.

Practice exercise. The endorphins that your brain releases during physical activity counteract the effects of sadness and favor your well-being. This is scientifically proven.

Recover or strengthen the bond with your family and friends, spend more time with them, let them listen and console you, and take the opportunity to get involved in some of their activities or interests.

Focus on the positive things of each day. Do a mental review of them at the end of the day when you get to sleep, and you will see that the picture is not as dark as it seems.

Pay attention again to your life project, consider new goals with realistic goals that you can meet at different times, and set some that are immediate to take advantage of the time you have now.

HOW TO REGAIN SELF-ESTEEM AFTER A BREAKUP

Ending a relationship can be painful, so I want to present some tips for you to learn how to regain self-esteem after a breakup.

If the relationship had been long or toxic, or the split was not by mutual agreement, it is likely that self-esteem has been somewhat affected and considerable healing time is required to overcome it.

RECOVER SELF-ESTEEM AFTER A BREAKUP

First of all, it is possible to understand what self-esteem is, since this is a word that we may hear frequently. Psychology dictionaries often define self-esteem as the assessment we make of ourselves.

If we do not enjoy good self-esteem, we can hardly live with balance at an emotional level, since the first step to achieve this is to accept ourselves.

HOW TO KNOW IF A HEART BREAK HAS AFFECTED YOUR SELF-ESTEEM

At the end of a relationship, there may be a situation in which emotional distress is experienced. But this does not have to mean the end of anything else in your life. However, it is also valid to recognize whether what is being lived at that time is just a couple of crises or a definitive break.

I UNDERSTAND WHY

In the case of the latter, we must understand that all the love we need lies in us, but we usually look for it outside, and this is one of the greatest mistakes we make after a breakup.

Dr. Jill Weber indicates that it is normal to feel confusion, sadness, or anger while losing a relationship. However, when relationships end, it is not necessarily uncommon, because we have all lived through these types of circumstances, but they are not the ones that define us.

On the contrary, even if a person is not in our near circle, life always continues and we must learn and continue our path of evolution. If you feel that some of the following items define you a bit, then that break is affecting your life and it is time to make changes.

LOW SELF-ESTEEM INDICATORS

- You feel that life has lost its meaning.
- You feel ugly when you look in the mirror and even think that no one else would fall in love with you anymore.
- You think that the person who has left was perfect and the only one on the planet for you.
- You take that person who has left as a benchmark to establish comparisons with the rest of the people you know.
- A carelessness arises in your personal image, and you no longer take care of your appearance.
- You do not feel enthusiasm for anything, have lost your motivation, and you are no longer interested in the activities that you loved before.
- You feel that pain does not allow you to have clear thoughts.

- You feel guilty about many things and think that, if you had acted differently, in certain situations, maybe that person would be by your side.

If you feel that any of these points identify you, then you must understand that loneliness can also be enjoyed, and that it is when we meet ourselves that true love arises.

STEPS TO REGAIN SELF-ESTEEM AFTER A BREAKUP

There is no magic formula to recover from a love break. It takes time. But the results are incredible, and the love you can feel for yourself after this experience will be much greater. To start, you must follow the following recommendations:

- Go through and live all the stages of grief after the break without trying to suppress them. It is preferable to tell someone you trust what you feel rather than shut up.
- Do not resort to evasion, just live it, because this is the best way to turn wounds into doors of light to be reborn. After this process you will be the only protagonist of your life.
- After living this moment, you will understand that your life does not depend on that person, nor should it revolve around it. You can make the most of your life by exploring all its potential.
- Establish a new routine, break with the old customs you had with that person.

I UNDERSTAND WHY

- Start the search inwards. Happiness is in you and not in someone else's life. Feeding love for yourself is a crucial step to see your value and understand why it wasn't in your best interest to be with toxic people.
- Avoid continuously talking about that person and what happened. It's fine to let off steam, but then we have to return our attention to ourselves to be our center again.
- Take care of yourself, love each other, take care of your appearance. Look in the mirror and see how beautiful you are from your own perception and not through someone else's eyes.
- You must take care of your physical and mental health. Get help from a therapist, life coach, pastor, etc. and develop all the activities that you loved before.
- Surround yourself with positive things. Forget the sentimental or sad songs at this time in your life; attract only joy.

11

Queen Michelle's Lesson

"I wanted him back. I went back and forth in my head from reasons why I should leave him alone to why I should call him and beg for him to come back home.

What was wrong with me?" asked Michelle

Michelle went on to tell me about all her many efforts to contact Derrick over the first two weeks after he left her. She called his family and friends, went to the gym that he usually played ball at, and attempted to contact him at the bank, but nothing worked until she ran into Derrick at Wal-Mart.

"At first I didn't notice it was him, until I saw those dusty-ass Nike slip-ons he always wears on his little quick errands. So I approached him.

'Derrick.'

At first he looked at me and didn't say anything, then he spoke.

'Michelle, hi," he stammered.

'Hey,' Michelle answered.

Tiffany, it's like my nerves were on pins and needles. I had so much I wanted to say I just was so scared.

'I thought I'd never see you again, Derrick... Why? What happened?'

'Can we not do this here?'

'I don't want to have this conversation here either, but you are ignoring me, and I haven't seen or heard from you for the past three weeks… Why, Derrick?'

'Look I'll call you tonight so we can talk,' Derrick answered.

'Derrick, please. I need answers now.'

'Michelle, I promise I will call you tonight.'

Then he walked away. He left me standing in the body wash aisle by myself with tears streaming down my cheeks. It hurt like hell to see him three weeks later with no explanation of why.

That night I stayed up all night waiting for that promised phone call. It never came.

About two weeks later at 1am in the morning, someone rang my doorbell.

When I looked through the peephole, it was Derrick.

I opened the door and he just burst out in tears.

'He's gone. He's gone, Shells.'

'Who, Derrick? What happened? I asked anxiously.

'My pops.'

Derrick was raised by his grandfather and saw his grandfather as his own father, who was absent Derrick's entire life. I felt for him, Tiffany. So I let him stay the night. He cried all night, and I took off the next day to be there for him because he needed me."

Michelle went on to tell me how that one night of allowing Derrick to sleep over due to being in mourning turned into a casual sex buddy arrangement for the next couple of months.

"We went from talking about marriage to casual sex whenever Derrick wanted it. I tried having the conversation about what led him to leave me, but he never wanted to talk about it."

Michelle went on to tell me that after Derrick started coming over to hang out and have sex for about a month or so, she eventually brought up the topic of them getting back together officially. But Derrick made it very clear that it was not the right time for them to get back together.

"It was tough for me to transition into his casual sex partner. I'm not sure if Derrick was talking to other females or not, but what I do know is that I wanted him back so badly. I wanted his love and his affection. It wasn't until one night after we were lying in the bed I asked Derrick what I would have to do to make him love me again, and he actually responded by saying, 'You don't know your place. You would have to learn your place, Michelle.'

I was stunned and shocked by his response. My initial reaction was to cuss him out and to tell him off, but I didn't. Instead I cried and begged for another chance, telling him I could do better.

It turned out 'better' meant following him. Like he said when we first spoke on that dating site. He was the head, the leader, and the provider.

So I told myself I was going to change my ways because I didn't have a problem with the man I love leading. But as I changed for him, I started getting sad and feeling depressed. You see, I was doing everything that he asked of me, and we still were only having casual sex. I eventually started turning to food and eating more. It first started with after everytime we had sex and when he would leave right after, I would go to the kitchen and eat something... anything. I started to feel worthless. And what didn't help is Derrick started becoming nasty. Making nasty comments about my weight. Making comments on how I dressed because I was feeling self-conscious about my weight gain and didn't feel comfortable wearing my usual wardrobe. I just felt like I was losing myself.

I UNDERSTAND WHY

Then last month I asked Derrick if we were ever going to get back together, and he told me that he would never take me seriously again because I don't know my value...

And that's why I'm here. I want to become the woman that he once loved. I want him back."

After hearing Michelle tell me her story of events that lead up to her wanting services, we worked on the steps to help her with rebuilding herself.

STEP 1: ACKNOWLEDGE

Step 1 was Michelle's most difficult step, as she was still in denial. Even though Derrick was telling Michelle that he didn't want her and being disrespectful to her, Michelle was holding on to the past when Derrick loved her. Michelle was only allowing herself to see the partial truth of their current situation.

"Tiffany, he has to love me. I know it. I know that you just can't fall out of love with someone overnight. I just need to help him remember what we had was real."

During this stage, I had Michelle go over her dating history. When I first met Michelle, she'd told me that when she originally met Derrick she was trying to get over her ex, Kevin. According to Michelle, Kevin didn't have any drive, and she felt for the two of them to be in their mid-thirties Kevin should have had his life a little more on track.

"So after Kevin I decided to make a list of what I wanted.

1. Religious
2. Ambitious
3. Family-oriented
4. Financially stable
5. Attractive
6. Good sex

7. Active in the community
8. Loves my family
9. Not afraid to settle down
10. Romantic"

"Michelle, you realize that you got everything that was on your list, right?" I asked.

Michelle looked at me, confused.

"Yup, you got what you asked for, so what's the problem?" I asked jokingly.

Michelle and I then discussed how she came up with her list. According to Michelle, she was writing her list based on everything that Kevin was not instead of making a list strictly about her needs, wants, and desires in her future husband.

"I never looked at it like that," Michelle admitted.

After talking about the importance of knowing what you want, Michelle went on to tell me that she always dated men just because they were available and interested.

"I never wanted to be a picky female and possibly miss out on the one for me," she explained.

"I mean, how do you know if you are saying no to your Mr. Right?" she asked.

Michelle went on to tell me about all her previous relationships and the various personalities of men she'd attracted and allowed in her life.

"Tiffany, I don't understand why I am having a hard time with keeping a man. I try my best to be what they want, and it never works out."

"Michelle, that's exactly what we need to work on," I answered.

I explained to Michelle that dating isn't about being a chameleon and just trying to blend in with whatever situation you are in.

Dating takes having standards and not just having standards for who you want, but more importantly, having standards for yourself.

Knowing who you are and what you are going to allow in your life and what you stand for.

During Step 1 Michelle eventually acknowledged that she didn't really know who she was and what she truly deserved in a relationship.

STEP 2: EMBRACE

After Michelle was able to accept the fact that her dating life had been on a roller coaster ride due to not having any real standards for herself, it was time to embrace the feelings of how being a chameleon in her relationships affected her life.

"In a way I feel like it silenced my voice and stunted my personal growth. Especially my relationship with Derrick. Everything has to be on his terms, and it's hard for me to continue this cycle we have going on."

I gave Michelle a journal and told her to write down all her feelings after she had any interaction with Derrick. Each week when Michelle and I would meet, we would go over the journal entries and discuss her honest feelings. Michelle's topics went from their sex life, which at this time was all about making sure Derrick was pleased, to the lack of respect Derrick had when he would speak to her.

In the beginning of Step 2, Michelle struggled a little with how to truly embrace her feelings until one night Derrick found her journal and they got into a heated argument over how she felt.

"Tiffany, he was in a complete rage, as though he couldn't understand why I felt the way that I do. I don't understand how he can read my journal and not feel at least a little guilty about how he has been treating me. All he kept telling me is I will never be anything more than what I am now. And when I asked 'And what exactly am I now?' he answered, 'You are nothing more than an insecure female that will lick the sole of my shoe if I told you that would make me want to be with you.'"

That session, Michelle cried as she told me she kicked him out of her home and changed the locks and blocked his cell phone number.

Michelle then was able to embrace that over the years she allowed herself to shrink herself and lose her dignity and respect for herself. Michelle journaled her disappointment with herself as she felt that she so easily gave up her crown in the hopes that the return would be love.

STEP 3: ACCEPTANCE

Once Michelle embraced her feelings regarding how she allowed herself to be treated in her failed relationships with men who weren't deserving of her time or energy, she worked on accepting the woman she is now.

One of the assignments I gave Michelle was called the ugly honest truth.

This assignment is when you reflect over your life and you write down everything that you see and feel about yourself. The good, the bad, and the ugly.

The second part of this assignment is during your day you have to work on everything that you wrote down and then finish the sentence at the end of the night on what you did to make that statement better.

I UNDERSTAND WHY

During this part of Michelle's healing process I had her read me some of her truths.

"My truth is I allowed myself to eat my emotions and I no longer feel attractive…. I joined a gym and decided to change my eating habits so I can get to a size that I am comfortable with.

My truth is I relied on my relationships to determine who I am… I made a list of my hobbies to figure out what I like for me and what makes me happy.

My truth is I gave up dancing and starting my own business because I wanted to keep my relationship… today I rejoined my old dance class.

My truth is I am a lot stronger than what I give myself credit for… I no longer will speak down on myself."

The goal behind this assignment was for Michelle to be honest with herself and work on accepting all aspects of herself while making sure she becomes the best version of herself.

On the last day of working on acceptance, Michelle started the session telling me how she and Derrick rekindled over the weekend and how he is back in her life.

"Oh okay, are you happy?" I asked.

"I mean, I missed him, but I'm still trying to figure everything out."

"Okay, I understand. There is nothing wrong with trying to figure out what is best for you, Michelle," I answered, hearing the shame in her voice.

"I don't know," Michelle responded. "It's not the same. I don't think my feelings are still there like they were before he exploded on me over my journal."

"My advice to you is let's continue these steps to your transformation. It's normal to second-guess your relationship, but what I want to make sure you get out of these sessions is that no matter what your transformation is, it's worth it, and it can help you with figuring out what you want from Derrick."

Michelle agreed, and we continued working on her rebuilding process.

STEP 4: FORGIVENESS

After Michelle was able to accept her truth, she needed to continue on working on healing from her hurt and pain. It was time for Michelle to forgive.

Initially, Michelle didn't see the point of having to forgive herself or anyone else, for that matter. But eventually Michelle was able to understand that letting go of hurt and pain and truly forgiving herself and others clears room in her soul for true happiness and love.

Because Michelle had previously expressed that dancing to music was a form of healing for herself, during this step, Michelle's assignment was to express her feelings through dance, a language that didn't have to be spoken, yet can still tell a story. Michelle picked out a song that she felt she connected with to describe her journey to her healing and transformation process and choreographed a dance to express her story.

According to Michelle, being able to tell her story through the artistry of dance was very powerful to her as she had let go of her love of music and dancing just to be loved by someone who was never deserving of her time or energy.

I UNDERSTAND WHY

STEP 5: LOVE ON YOURSELF—THE TRANSFORMATION

As Michelle worked daily to rebuild herself and transform into the woman she was no longer afraid to hide, she found herself working on her dreams of owning her own dance studio.

"I can't believe everything's coming together for me. After all I've been through I honestly never thought I would be able to say that I own my own dance studio," Michelle shrieked.

"Believe it, you worked hard to get here." I laughed.

"It's crazy. I always thought that I would need Derrick for the financial support. He's been offering to help me out financially, but it's not because he believes in my vision, but I think it's because he doesn't think I can do this on my own. I'm grateful that I have been able to stand on my own two feet and was able to turn the basement into a private air bnb space for extra income. That extra money has really helped me to be able to afford the downpayment for the dance studio space."

It didn't take Michelle long before she was able to have her dance studio up and running for the youth of her community. Not only did Michelle get her business going but she was able to also keep up with her healthy lifestyle and was in the best shape of her life.

"I just feel so liberated. I live my life the way that I please. I am unapologetically me. I'm just so grateful that all this hard work that I have put into taking control of my life has truly paid off."

"Well, your grand opening is this weekend. Are you ready?" I asked excitedly.

"Yes, I'm ready! I can't wait to tell you all about it," Michelle exclaimed.

My next session with Michelle I thought I would have been greeted by a burst of uncontrollable energy, but instead I was greeted with a somber hello.

"Hi, Tiffany."

"Hey, Michelle, everything okay? How was the grand opening?"

"It was nice. It went well, a lot of people showed up and signed up their children."

"Well that's great! Right?" I asked.

"Yeaah… I'm sorry, Tiffany. I just have a lot on my mind."

"Feel free to share if you want to talk about it."

"It's Derrick. The day after the grand opening he asked me out. No, let me correct that. He stated that we could be a couple again."

I looked at Michelle and tilted my head in confusion.

"Yeah, he wanted to come over the night of the grand opening, but I told him I had plans and I wasn't available that night. He texted me nonstop all night trying to figure out where I was and who I was with.

The next day he called me, which I thought was weird because he hasn't called my phone in a long time, and when I answered the phone he blurted out,

'Michelle, I was thinking of how you really wanted to be with me and I agree. We should make us official again.'"

Michelle went on to tell me how she was completely confused as she has not mentioned trying to be with Derrick in months.

"Tiffany, I swear when he came back around this last time, something was off. I wasn't impressed nor pressed for him. I just been working on me like you said, and I don't think Derrick is my type. He is a self serving pompous asshole and I think I just allowed him back because that's originally what I wanted, but now things have changed. I love this version of myself that I have worked hard for to heal, restore, rebuild, and transform. What do I do?"

I asked Michelle two simple questions.

1. Do you know what you bring to the table?
2. Do you agree with what he thinks he brings to the table?

Michelle looked at me, confused. "What he thinks he brings to the table? What do you mean?"

I then suggested to Michelle that she give Derrick the chance to tell her what he thinks he brings to the table, and Michelle will be able to make her decision from there.

Our next session I asked Michelle if she'd had her conversation with Derrick.

Michelle told me that Derrick showed up to her home with two dozen roses, and before he could walk in, while he stood in the doorway, Michelle said, "So Derrick, I thought about what we spoke about the other day regarding us being in a relationship. I was just wondering … why should I want to be with you."

12

The Rainbow at the End of the Storm

> "No matter what happens, or how bad it seems today, life does go on, and it will get better tomorrow."
> Maya Angelou

6 REASONS WHY BEING FRIENDS WITH BENEFITS WITH YOUR EX ISN'T A GOOD IDEA

Some of us might think that the best way of getting an ex back is sleeping with them. But it is probably not the best strategy, as it might end up doing more harm than good. The problem is that more often than not, you or your ex will resent each other for the way things are playing out. Unfortunately, while being friends with benefits with your ex sounds amazing, usually things don't go as planned. This type of relationship leads to the destruction of your physical relationship and friendship.

I UNDERSTAND WHY

WHAT ARE FRIENDS WITH BENEFITS?

Friends with benefits mean that you are continually sleeping with someone—your ex—without being in a committed relationship with them. Many people make the mistake of starting a friend with benefits relationship so their ex can become a partner again, but this almost never ends well. Why?

Because usually the ex just wants sex and no relationship. So you get your ex back in your life but not necessarily in the way you wanted. Besides, because you agree to sleep with your ex without being in a committed relationship, they know they can take advantage of you. In the end, they are not interested in anything else to do with you. After all, they only said yes to sleeping with you, not getting back together. Here are more reasons why being friends with benefits with your ex is a bad idea.

JEALOUSY

Because you remain "friends" with your ex, you are probably going to see him/her flirting or going out with other people. While for some people, this might not be a problem, if you are still in love with your ex, it can trigger jealousy, even if you logically know you are not in an exclusive relationship.

RESENTMENT

After you sleep with your ex, it will often lead to further angst and confusion about what it means and where you go. You have to believe me, you will have this thought: "I slept with my ex, I still love him/her, why can't we just be together?" The fact that you ended up friends with benefits means you both are struggling to break off a toxic relationship defined by up and down cycles.

THINGS CHANGE

Even if you start off on the same page, things change. It is an old cliché: two people start off wanting just sex, free of a commitment, then one person wants more. Eventually, you will enter a gray area of feels, which can cloud your judgment. So even if you think it is emotionless, things can get confusing. You will have certain expectations, and there is a good chance you will get hurt again.

YOU CAN GET ATTACHED

Having good sex might be the perfect excuse to gravitate toward someone we have familiarity with. This can prevent us from finding someone new. If you want to move on and meet someone, you can't get caught up in the comfort of sex with your ex.

YOUR EX MIGHT THINK YOU ARE INTO HIM/HER AGAIN

Your ex might think that you want to be with him/her again. Next thing you know, you are once again in a relationship you did not wish to be in. Even if you assume your ex knows that you only want sex, things can go from zero to a 100 real quick.

VULNERABLE

Finally, thinking that you have no feelings and that you can have just sex with your ex is delusional. Although there are exceptions, the truth is that most people in this situation are definitely feeling something. Having sex makes you vulnerable again. Being intimate with someone you used to feel strongly about will expose you to deal with everything on an emotional basis

HOW TO BREAK SOUL TIES AFTER A BREAKUP?

Forming a deep emotional bond with another person is powerful. A soul tie can influence or manipulate you, and it can even stop you from having future relationships. The only way you can move on is by breaking soul ties.

But what is a soul tie?

A soul tie is having a spiritual connection with another person. It is formed after an exceptional emotional relationship. It usually comes after being physically intimate with someone. It is common to have this spiritual bond with your previous partner because that person was part of your life for a long time.

Unfortunately, an emotional connection does not end when you end a relationship.

When you are in love with someone, it seems like you are tied to that person, because your hopes and dreams were tied to that person. When you imagine your future, you think about him or her. And now that you break up, you feel lost because that person anchored you.

Invisible soul ties can stay long after the relationship has ended. It is common to obsess about your ex or even imagine or hearing him/her in your head. These symptoms may impact your current or future relationship.

The good news is that it is unnecessary to have a big exorcism to set you free because, more often than not, you are suffering from a broken heart. This means that it is possible to break a soul tie to move on with your life.

4 STEPS TO BREAK A SOUL TIE

1. ACCEPTANCE

The first step to break a soul tie is to accept your new situation. It is vital to acknowledge that your relationship has ended with no hope or wish to continue. When you accept your new place, you are freeing yourself from the past.

You need to live in the present. I won't lie to you, it won't be easy, but it helps if you put in place new rules that will put down the basis for a new relationship with your ex. Remember, these rules are there to protect you from further damage.

2. CREATE A PROPER ENVIRONMENT

The second step is to build a new structure that empowers you. It is critical to creating a healthy environment that will both motivate and move you toward your goal. Make sure to create an environment that will help you regain your independence. Remove all the provocations to stay connected with your ex. Remember, now it is time to work in your inner healing.

3. FORGIVE

It is often the most challenging step to take. You need to comprehend that forgiveness is for you, not the other person. When you forgive, you get your power back.

Forgiveness is not about condoning bad behavior. It is the only way to be free and move on. Resentment and bitterness can keep your soul tied, and when you forgive, you release it. This also means you need to forgive yourself for your decisions, which is usually hard to do.

4. REMOVE PHYSICAL OBJECTS

The last step is to remove any physical objects that might connect you to your ex. This should include photos and gifts. Please note that objects are symbols of the tie, and you need to remove them from your life.

Finally, there is hope if you find yourself in an unhealthy soul tie. You can always be restored as long as you acknowledge that a new life is available to live in freedom and happiness again.

5 WAYS TO ADD TO YOUR INCOME AFTER A DIVORCE/BREAKUP

Without any doubt, the most devastating cost of divorce is its impact on the family, but it is important to understand that divorce can also be financially damaging. In most cases, your income is affected because you lost the financial support of your significant other.

The best way to deal with this is to be prepared.

First, you should expect a lower income after the divorce is final. Develop a budget based on needs, and don't forget to adjust your expenses to stay within your post-divorce income.

Make sure to include all sources of income including spousal and child support, but keep in mind that they won't last forever, and don't forget to add investment income if you have it.

5 WAYS TO EARN EXTRA MONEY

As a single parent, it is hard to find time to take on a second or even third full-time job. The good news is that there are ways to earn extra cash in your spare time.

Here are five simple ways to do it.

1. GET A REAL ESTATE LICENSE

Getting a real estate license has many unquestionable benefits that are well worth the time, effort, and money. Here are five benefits of a real estate license:

1. You can earn extra income.
2. You will gain access to more profitable deals.
3. Your professional network will expand.
4. Your business knowledge and skills will increase.
5. You can earn good commissions with every sale.

Becoming a real estate agent will give you the freedom to set your hours and earn a living by selling properties.

I UNDERSTAND WHY

2. BECOME A NOTARY

If you enjoy handling legal documents and guiding signers to complete an official agreement, becoming a notary can be a rewarding job. If you are looking for a way to work from home or a part-time job to get you out of the house for a few hours, you should consider becoming a notary.

A notary commission can open the door to more than a dozen additional money-making opportunities. When you become a notary you are showing that you have integrity and that gives you an advantage in your competition.

3. TRAVEL AGENT

If you love to travel, you are good at logistics and enjoy sales, then becoming a travel agent might be a good option. Your commissions will ensure a good salary.

There are two ways you can work from home as a travel agent:

1. Working independently as a travel agent. In this case, you are responsible for the business; this includes creating your website or blog, finding clients, advertising, and forming a relationship with different travel companies.
2. Working as a travel agent for a host agency. Here you will be self-employed. You will need to do training, but you will have more support from the agency.

4. AIRBNB

If you have an extra room or a second home to rent, you can become an Airbnb host. Most people think that becoming a host involves a lot of risks, but it is a simple, stable way to make extra money on the side.

Airbnb hosting can be a very profitable side-hustle that doesn't take up that much of your time. You can do it even if:

- You are just renting a room
- You only have an extra room in your home
- You don't have that much extra time

5. LIFE INSURANCE AGENT

You can make good money by selling life insurance. Some life insurance agents are making over $100,000 per year. Many make a lot more than that! You can expect to earn $2,000-$5,000 per month starting.

How much you earn will depend on the products you sell and how hard you are willing to work. The good thing is that you can start at home and you have the freedom to choose your hours.

6. ONLINE TUTORING

Online tutoring isn't new, but it's a terrific time to become a tutor right now. It allows you to work from the comfort of your home. One of the best things about being an online tutor is that you can make your schedule. With online tutoring, you get to choose when and where you want to work and it pays between $10-$15/hour.

Besides, it's a rewarding experience since you can help students learn. When you teach, you're making your students' life more manageable, helping them grow.

To start as an online tutor, you need to determine your requirements. This means you need to have an explicit understanding of the industry and skills you want to deliver to learners.

Finally, you need to choose the right platform for your online courses. There are two options available:

1. Sign up with existing tutoring websites
2. Create your tutoring platform

Decide which one is better for your needs. Remember, tutoring is fun and rewarding, as well as a flexible business to get into.

7. FIVERR

A terrific way to start earning money in any profession is on Fiverr. Fiverr has a different approach than other freelance platforms, but it's a great starting point for many freelancers.

What Is Fiverr?

Fiverr is a platform for exchanging services online. In this platform, you can buy and sell whatever you can provide digitally. It has been on the market for more than ten years, and every 5 seconds, there's one service purchased.

One of the main benefits of Fiverr is that you aren't required to talk to your customers on the phone at any time, as is the case with other platforms. So even if English isn't your primary language, you can work on the forum.

Starting to sell on Fiverr is easy and free to join. Once you are registered, you need to create a gig. A gig is a method that's used to sell services on the platform.

How much you can earn on Fiverr depends on several factors. But you can expect 100-300 dollars for the first month using the different options for additional gigs that Fiverr has.

BOTTOM LINE

To survive emotionally and financially after a divorce is possible. Believe me, earning extra money is something that can change your life. Money can buy you the freedom and it can improve many areas of your life, including having less stress from living alone paycheck to paycheck.

Knowing that you are capable of taking care of yourself and your family is the first step to becoming better, stronger, and more confident. Don't be afraid—you can and you will do it!

I UNDERSTAND WHY

THE POWER OF CHANGING YOUR HABITS ONE AT A TIME

"The secret of change is to focus all of your energy, not on fighting the old, but on building the new."
Socrates

The number one reason why most people fail with habit development is that it is impossible to change several habits at the same time.

It is not easy to develop new habits as we are used to doing the same thing over and over again.

If you want to change your habits, you need a lot of mental strength and engagement. When you focus on changing multiple habits at the same time, it is easy to exhaust your willpower. And if this happens you will eventually give up.

The good news is that there is a simple solution to this problem, and that is to change one habit at a time.

WHY IS IT IMPORTANT TO CHANGE ONE HABIT AT A TIME?

When you focus on changing one habit at a time, it can help you develop a daily routine.

For example, say you want to lose weight. A daily habit would be to start eating more fruits and vegetables.

The key is to start small. It is not a good idea to start going to the gym three hours daily, eating only one apple a day, and stop eating desserts. You will feel overwhelmed and in most cases, you will not be able to follow this routine.

Start by eating one fruit daily instead of a dessert, then eat a salad at lunch.

When you focus on a single habit at a time, you can create a new routine. It is easier to keep up with this new routine instead of trying to do multiple actions at once.

6 WAYS TO CHANGE YOUR HABITS

On average, it takes 66 days before a new habit becomes a routine. So focus on a single habit at a time, and you will be able to make a permanent change. Here are six ways to do it.

1. IDENTIFY YOUR GOAL

The most important thing you need to do is to identify what you want to change.

For example, if you want to be more physically active, the habit you need to focus on is to walk at least 3 times per week for 20 minutes.

2. FIND YOUR MOTIVATION

As we mentioned before, changing habits is hard, so you need to know why you are doing it. Write down the reasons why you want to change.

So if you are feeling down or overwhelmed, review your list of reasons and find the motivation to keep going.

I UNDERSTAND WHY

3. SUBSTITUTE YOUR BAD HABIT

It is important to understand that you don't eliminate a bad habit, you replace it. If you want to change a bad habit, you need to:

- Identify the behavior you want to change
- Understand what triggers your bad habits
- Make small changes

For example, if you want to stop smoking and you only smoke when you drink, stop going to bars. Don't forget to have a plan of what you are going to do when you get the urge to smoke, like chewing gum or doing breathing exercises instead.

4. CELEBRATE YOUR WINS

After a month of committing to the new habit, reward yourself with something you like. This will give you the motivation to stick with your new routine.

5. TRACK YOUR PROGRESS

It is important to track your progress every day. It is a good idea to break down your goal into smaller tasks. This will help you track those small steps daily.

6. MAKE A PLAN

It is not enough to say you are going to change a habit within a period; you need to make a plan. Create a plan with each step of how you are going to change it. This will help you accomplish your goals faster.

REMEMBER

Focusing 100 percent on one single habit is the best way to create a new routine. Having this dedication allows you to keep your strength and willpower to conquer your hesitation and laziness when you are not in the mood to follow your goals.

Remember, don't try to change your life overnight. Instead, focus on making one small change at a time. With time, those small changes will transform your routine. Just don't give up!

5 WAYS TO RECOVER FROM PHYSICAL AND EMOTIONAL ABUSE

Both men and women are susceptible to physical and emotional abuse, especially within intimate relationships. Those who have suffered it are deeply hurt. Without undergoing an appropriate healing process, their future relationships will be permanently taken apart. The victim of constant emotional abuse has many self-destructive problems. These symptoms are similar to those of post-traumatic stress disorder (PTSD) victims, including:

- Unwanted and upsetting memories
- Nightmares
- Flashbacks
- Disturbing bodily reactions
- Anxiety
- Blame
- Guilt

I UNDERSTAND WHY

- Isolation
- Helplessness
- Watchfulness
- Frightened responses

HOW TO RECOGNIZE IF YOU HAVE BEEN ABUSED

It is essential to understand that abuse can come in many forms. Emotional abuse is just as damaging as physical abuse, and most times, they happen together.

If you are not sure if it is happening to you, here are some of the most common signs:

- Punishing you
- Ridiculing you
- Insults
- Name-calling
- Yelling
- Making you question your sanity
- Trying to control your life
- Making subtle or overt threats
- Isolating you from friends and family
- Invading your privacy
- Making you feel guilty

The most important thing you need to comprehend is that it is not your fault if you have been physically and emotionally abused. Don't forget that emotional abuse is NOT normal, but the effects of abuse are.

If you have been in an abusive relationship and it has come to an end, you might be wondering: "What should I do?" Here are some effective ways to recover if you are a survivor of emotional and physical abuse.

TIFFANY SMITH

1. LET GO OF SHAME

If you have been in an unhealthy relationship lasting far too long, one of the biggest parts of recovery is forgiveness. You need to forgive yourself and let go of shame. You need to stop beating yourself up and thinking that it is your fault. Sometimes it is easier to forgive the abuser than to forgive yourself. It is common to be angry at yourself for staying. You need to forgive yourself for how long it took you to be able to move on.

2. TAKE YOUR TIME

There are five stages to an abusive relationship:

1. The relationship starts
2. The abuse begins
3. The abuse is recognized
4. You end the relationship and leave the abuse
5. Healing begins

You must understand that healing from emotional and verbal abuse takes time. First, there is the aftershock, then the doubt, and finally regaining your self-confidence.

3. MAKING SENSE OF THE ABUSE

It is challenging to try to make sense of the abuse and what to do after. It is totally normal to experience confusion and fear over where to start. An excellent place to start can be therapy or having a life coach. With either therapy or a life coach, you can learn to ask for help.

If it is possible, confront the abuser and their actions to start healing. If you can't do it in person, write a letter and let him/her know how you feel. Attend relevant workshops, classes, or seminars, or do a quick search online and look for local organizations, communities, and support groups.

4. CREATE HEALTHY BOUNDARIES

Creating healthy boundaries is crucial to building strong relationships. Having healthy boundaries means knowing and understanding what your limits are. The first step is to determine your physical, emotional, mental, and spiritual limits. Decide what you can tolerate and accept and what makes you feel uncomfortable or stressed.

Watch out for two key feelings that are red flags: discomfort and resentment. When a person acts in a way that makes you feel uncomfortable, he or she is probably violating or crossing a boundary.

5. REBUILD YOUR STORY

Gaslighting is when the abuser is attempting to change your reality by altering how you see yourself. Abusive, false narratives are common, and they affect the way you see yourself. The lies that the abuser told about you will continue to impact the way you see yourself. The good news is that once the abuser is out of your life, you can rebuild your story.

BOTTOM LINE

It is important to understand that being out of that abusive relationship can feel more frightening than good, and that is normal. Keep in mind that's what your abuser wants.

THE LAW OF ATTRACTION AND HOW TO MANIFEST YOUR DESTINY AFTER A BREAKUP

> "What you think, you become. What you feel, you attract. What you imagine, you create."
> Buddha

Do you think the Law of Attraction can change destiny? The simple answer is yes. Destiny, unlike fate, is not set in stone. Destiny is based on life lessons and opportunities. When you know how to use the Law of Attraction, you can learn how to bring more positive opportunities and experiences into your life.

To have a happier, fuller relationship, you need to use the right tools, and you need a positive mindset. If you want to use the Law of Attraction to modify your love destiny, it is important to learn how to send a clear message to the universe regarding what you want.

Here are 10 steps to manifest your destiny after a breakup.

I UNDERSTAND WHY

1. KNOW EXACTLY WHAT YOU WANT

When you don't know what you want, you can't do anything to make it happen. To manifest something and change your destiny, you must know what you wish for.

Write down at least 20 to 25 things you want to manifest. Remember to be specific and positively list the attributes.

2. FOLLOW YOUR HEART

The best way to do the above list is by following your heart. Your heart is tender, loving, and it will probably tell you what you want. When you follow your heart, you will probably make the right choices instead of making self-serving ego-dominant decisions.

3. CONNECT WITH YOUR DREAMS AND GOALS

If you want the Law of Attraction to work, you need to connect with your dreams and goals. Not just set goals to be specific. This means you need to think about what you want.

For example, describe what kind of person would be your **IDEAL** partner, and what would your **DREAM** relationship be like.

4. ASK THE UNIVERSE

Now that you have your list, it is time to let the universe know what you want. You have to keep in mind that the universe can only help you get what you want when you are clear in your desires.

It is key to not leave what you receive up to chance; ask for what you want. You can do this by:

- Praying
- Meditating
- Visualizing
- Vision boards
- Writing a letter

You can choose one or all of the above options, but make sure to ask the universe for what you want at least once a day.

5. CONNECT WITH YOUR EMOTIONS

Did you know that emotions are powerful energy? If you want to change your destiny and manifest your desires, you need to develop methods to control your emotions.

Establish a passion for who you are and what you are here to share. Connect emotionally with your desires.

6. USE YOUR IMAGINATION

To attract your desires and change your destiny, you need to use your imagination. You need to see it clearly in your mind, feel it and think about it so much that you can "taste it"; then you will attract what you want.

7. WORK TOWARD YOUR GOALS

To attract what you want, it is imperative to work toward your goals. Remember, manifesting is just the art of co-creating with

I UNDERSTAND WHY

the universe. When you work toward your goals, you are increasing your opportunities of receiving what you want.

Write down three actions you can do to bring you one step closer to your goal.

8. STAY TUNED

To manifest your destiny, you need to stay in touch with who you are. Make sure to align yourself with your thoughts, feelings, and actions. It is key to visualize yourself as one with your goal and act as if your goal has already been achieved.

Remember to be aware of environmental influences, as negative people can affect your results. Always surround yourself with people who help you deliver the best in you.

9. FOCUS ON SELF-LOVE

After a breakup or divorce, it is extremely important to focus on self-love.

If you want to be more fulfilled sexually, romantically, or emotionally, you need to love yourself.

When you love yourself, you automatically attract more love in your life and have more loving, satisfying relationships.

10. TRUST THE PROCESS

Throughout your journey, you may question if the Law of Attraction and manifesting your destiny work. You might get frustrated and demoralized.

Never sit down and wonder when things are going to happen. If you do that, you are not trusting the process. When you have doubts, you are sending the message to the universe to prove manifesting doesn't work.

Many times when people start thinking about what they want (like money), they automatically go to thinking about the lack of it, which (like the doubting) is counterproductive.

To see results and manifest your destiny, you must trust the process.

Repeat this every time you find yourself doubting: *"I know the universe has my back and I am getting closer and closer to my desired destiny every day."*

Say this phrase every day!

JOURNALING TOPICS TO ASSIST WITH HEALING AFTER A BREAKUP

The ending of a relationship is painful, whether you were left or the leaver. It is a loss, the end of a dream of what could have been and what was. During my divorce, one of the best tools I had to heal my broken heart was writing in a journal. Breakup emotions are overwhelming, and you can find it challenging to think when you have so many feelings at once. An excellent way to process these emotions and start recovering is to try journaling. Are you wondering if journaling really helps after a breakup? Studies have shown that writing down how you are coping with your breakup reduces post-breakup loneliness and distress, as it enables you to define your self-confidence.

Experts agree that regularly journaling about your breakup can help you heal faster. Writing down your feelings is a great

I UNDERSTAND WHY

way to practice letting go. It gives you the chance to release your thoughts and emotions that have developed. Writing particularly about your breakup is the most healing way to journal. When you do this, you are processing emotions and clarifying your thoughts. The truth is that when you have many complicated feelings, it can be challenging to differentiate your thoughts. When you sit down to journal, you are allowing your mind to slow down and think about different elements of your current situation. To learn where to start, keep reading!

ANALYZE WHAT WAS GOOD FROM THE RELATIONSHIP

It is time to think about all the things that you liked about the relationship. Start by writing down what you miss most about your ex. This could be:

- Trust
- Understanding one another
- Communication
- Gratitude
- Excitement

ANALYZE WHAT WAS BAD FROM THE RELATIONSHIP

Writing down this section in your journal will stop you from getting back together when you read the answers to these questions.

If you read the answers and decide the relationship is worth another try, it is your choice, but be brutally honest.

- Why did we break up?
- What didn't I like about him?
- What didn't I like about my life with him/her?
- How did my relationship limit my life?
- What are the best things about my life without him/her?

Remember, a good relationship is based on being able to to discuss a problem and reach a solution calmly.

ANALYZE WHAT YOU HAVE LEARNED ABOUT THE RELATIONSHIP

Challenging times have within them an opportunity to learn and grow. When you focus on how you can grow, you shift out of a victim mentality. Try to answers questions such as:

- What did I learn from the relationship?
- How can I improve my next relationship?
- How can I grow from this breakup?

It is essential to understand that no one is ever 100 percent "right" or "wrong," so treat your next relationship like a democracy, not a dictatorship.

I UNDERSTAND WHY

KEEP A PLAYLIST OF YOUR FAVORITE SONGS

Writing about your favorite songs will evoke the mood you are in right now. When you hear a song that triggers a strong memory, write down how you feel. Do you feel inspired, happy, sad, or contemplative?

WRITE ABOUT YOUR STRENGTHS AND WEAKNESSES

Make a list of three qualities you have that you consider weaknesses and explore how they affect your relationship. For instance, you might think you are jealous. Write down how you will change this behavior in the future. See jealousy or any other relationship issue as a window of opportunity to gain clarity.

PRACTICE GRATITUDE

Being grateful is the key to start healing your broken heart. List five things that you are thankful for, then expand on each one, describing it in detail, perhaps at a particular moment in time.

You might be grateful for:

- Having time for yourself
- The ability to do whatever you want, whenever you want to
- No more fighting
- You have the whole bed to yourself
- You don't have to deal with his/her family or friends

- You can stop walking on eggshells
- You can go on dates with yourself

BOTTOM LINE

These are great journaling topics to start with after a breakup. Journaling is the best way to get to know yourself even better. Writing in a journal will help you find your strengths to develop a plan for your next relationship.

COMMIT TO HEALTHY HABITS POST-DIVORCE OR BREAKUP

It's no secret that "breaking up is hard to do," and even more so when it comes to dissolving a marriage through divorce. As women, we can be especially hard on ourselves during these difficult times of transition, adding even more stress and anxiety to an already stressful time. It's all too common to try to ease the stress by vegging out, withdrawing from others, and reaching for the most satisfying junk food at hand. Here are some healthy habits you can concentrate on post-divorce or breakup that will not only help in your healing process but also keep you functioning happily and healthily. It's all about focusing on you, on your love and appreciation for yourself, and treating your body and mind with respect and self-love.

I UNDERSTAND WHY

HEALTHY HABITS TO EMPLOY AFTER A BAD BREAKUP

HEALTHY EATING

A healthy diet tops the list because it is probably the best thing you can do to care for both your body *and* mind while going through a divorce. Instead of overindulging in junk foods or alcohol, focus on getting all the good stuff on your plate each day. This isn't the time to jump into an overly restrictive diet, either. Fill your fridge—and consequently your meals and snacks—with healthy fruits and veggies, lean proteins, and healthy fats. By filling up on the good stuff first, you'll find that cravings for less nutritious foods wane considerably. At the same time, if you do decide to indulge, do it moderately and without guilt. Fully enjoy that cookie, bowl of ice cream, or that glass or two of wine, and then move on.

GET ACTIVE

Breakups are *depressing,* there's no doubt about that, and it's far too easy to withdraw and opt for binge watching Netflix instead of getting out and getting active. But that's exactly what you should be doing! Regular exercise is an incredible stress-reliever, self-confidence builder, mood-booster, and more. Hit the gym, take up a new exercise class, call up some girlfriends and go for a hike, take a spin around the neighborhood on a bicycle—anything that you enjoy and that gets your muscles moving. The idea is to include some kind of movement into your routine *each day.*

REST + RECOVER

An essential piece of the puzzle is allowing yourself to rest and recover as well. Sleep is your body's reset process, and you need it to be able to function at your highest level all of the time, but especially while you're emotionally and mentally recovering. Make sure while you're going through a divorce or breakup that you are paying attention to getting enough quality sleep each night.

REACH OUT TO FRIENDS AND FAMILY

Your friends and family *want* to be there for you during this difficult time, so let them! They're called your support system for a reason—lean on them! Go out and do things that you enjoy, talk things out with them if that feels productive, or try something new and allow it to distract you for a while. Allowing your friends to be there for you when you need it will reinforce your feelings of self-confidence and self-esteem and help you remember how much you are loved.

DON'T FORGET SELF-CARE

Self-care might be the last thing on your mind when dealing with a difficult breakup, but don't let it fall by the wayside! Seriously. You need to be the biggest reminder to yourself how much you deserve to be loved and cared for. You can do something simple like taking a hot shower and taking the time to do your hair and makeup so you feel beautiful and ready to take on your day, or it can be something more practical like taking the time to schedule that dentist appointment you've been putting off.

The bottom line is this: ending a marriage or going through a tough breakup can be incredibly stressful on your mind and body. The healing process means that you will need to take plenty of time to focus on and care for yourself in the healthiest ways possible. Fuel your body with healthy food, boost your mood with daily movement, rest and recover your mind and body, get reacquainted with yourself again, chase and conquer your dreams, and nourish your soul with friends, family and self-care.

Epilogue

When years have passed and time has come and gone, you'll realize that you were always enough. As a matter of fact, you really didn't need anyone to make you whole and worthy.

You've walked through a stony path, a really tough road. But that's exactly why you're a stronger woman. You've been grieving, and that's okay, but now, you're rising. The woman you are right now is a combination of all your scars, yet you rose. Looking back, things could have been harder, and I could have chosen to stay in a dark place. But getting to where I am now was a decision, more than just a feeling, an intentional decision. And it's the exact same thing you're doing right now, making the decision to thrive.

You're taking time to heal, acknowledging that you were hurt, embracing the reality of choosing a life without him, accepting your new status (which, by the way, is still really cool), letting go of the one who hurt you because it's also important for your healing, and ultimately, loving yourself.

Now that you're starting a new life, sis, getting on with those goals is your surest bet to making the best of this life. Remember, you're now in a place of self-love and appreciation. So it's time to get on with doing things all for yourself. It's a whole new chapter! Remember the woman you always thought you were going to be

I UNDERSTAND WHY

before the world told you what to be instead? When you were a carefree little girl. You're right in the place now where you can be her, unfettered. So it's exciting to think that you're chasing those goals, building that life you really want. It's exciting to see you falling in love with yourself all over again, choosing yourself over everything else. How does that feel? Let me guess, liberating and wholesome. I know because I've been where you are right now, finally healing and getting in touch with yourself, and it's the best feeling in the world. So what's that thing you've always wanted to do? Go hard on it!

I know this is a process. It's not all over yet. It was never going to be all done in a day. True healing takes a while, sometimes, a long while. But what's great is that you're already on the path to it and that you're eventually going or get there. You're probably pausing for moments and asking yourself, "wait a minute, can I do this?" But look at you, you're doing it already, and that's why you're here right now, looking past the hurts and betrayals, rising above the disappointments, choosing yourself. Now, isn't that something? And don't you dare, get back to that place of guilt, that place where you're blaming yourself for everything that went wrong; this wasn't your fault. You're done with that mindset.

And you're done holding on to it, somehow hoping that it's still going to work out. This is going to take another while. But you're getting used to it one step at a time. You're getting used to knowing that that relationship is your past, and you're not going back there. You're getting used to knowing that it's over. You realize that you were always better than a relationship that hurts you anyway. But I can relate to where you are right now, that somewhat still difficult place. Even after how far you've come. Some days, your mind still goes back to it, and you're wondering what could have been. I'm going to give you an answer, sis, nothing! Nothing could have been. I mean, nothing could have been better than the fact that you're rising, slowly but surely. Nothing could have been better than this peace you're finally finding.

And if you already had kids in your relationship, I'm positive you're not fretting about how to make that work. Having kids together can really make the whole process even more challenging. But now that you've chosen to move on with your life, you're going to see how definitely possible it can be. It's working, right? After all these chapters, I believe you're in a better place to stay off all the drama and just really be a great mom to your kids, co-parenting with your ex like a boss. Because well, now you know how to do it and kill it. I see you in my mind's eye, being an amazing single mom, expertly walking your children through it all, being able to keep them stable and happy. And most of all, being able to keep yourself happy. What could be better?

Now, you're queening! I know the anger still comes, those moments when you're thinking about how far you went, all the sacrifices you made, all the investments you put into it. Who would have thought it would end like this? Who would have thought he wouldn't be in your life until forever? Who would have thought you'd have to deal with all that pain? But again, who would have thought you'd come this far? Who would have thought that in spite of it all, you'd still be here, thriving? So the thing is, life comes with all these uncertainties. Our ability to rise up, face them, and still rise above them is what makes the whole difference.

So in the midst of all the crazy emotions you're feeling, don't stop moving and certainly, don't stop rising. So all that free time you probably have now? Put it to good use, girl. And no, Netflix, ice-cream, and chill are not really the thing. You know why? You might find yourself in that unhealthy mental place again. Now isn't the time to sit around doing that, now is the time to build.

The absolute best thing you can do for yourself right now is to take care of yourself and live for you. Get those endorphins alive by exercising. You need those chemicals a lot to keep separating you from the sad and lonely person you once were. And keep your beauty sleep alive because no one deserves it more than you, and your mind needs it now more than ever.

A quick secret, taking care of yourself is going to have you looking hotter than ever. Don't know, but I'm all up for that, and you should be too; you didn't come this far to just let it slide. After all, looking good has always been a great way to get back in your elements. So, you're not letting yourself fall apart; you're building yourself. Again, I acknowledge that it's been a tough process, but I admire your courage to get this far.

So here you are, walking right towards your perfect place, your place of perfect healing, the place where nothing hurts anymore. And I'm delighted that I get to share in this journey, that you let me have a part in it. Now, you're breaking that soul tie and building new routines and creating habits that serve you, and most importantly, building your life! The rainbow is here.

And when it finally happens, when all the pain is truly gone, you'll know, and it'll feel like a breeze. How?

The memories won't matter anymore. They'll become more events from a story you used to know. No doubt, you might still feel tiny trickles of sadness, but it's not going to be the feeling that has you wanting to curl in bed and grind your teeth and soak your pillow. You're past that now.

And guess what again. You're soon going to lose all that interest in talking about your marriage and divorce. Now that's a boss girl thing. Yes, talking about it so often helped you to process it in the past. Because well, you wanted supporters who would sympathize with you. So I'm sure you've caught yourself one time too many trying to make every conversation everywhere about your divorce, somehow trying to always bring it in. But truly healing means you're no longer interested in that, you really don't care anymore, you don't even want to go there. Now, you have a lot of other important things to talk about, things that look like the amazing new life you're building. Plus, you're going to find yourself being super selective, cautious of where you talk about your marriage and divorce. You're no longer throwing the conversation around. Are you here yet? Take your time

I'm going to tell you one more thing about finally getting into your right place. You'll start recognizing, again, what was actually good about your marriage, even though it ended badly. There definitely was something good about your relationship, even if it was a single thing. There must have been good days and appreciable character traits. I mean, that's about the only reason you could have married your ex. A bad breakup can have you dissing the whole relationship just to console yourself, and somehow, it really works, albeit momentarily, to stop the sting. But the truth is, you were in that relationship for however long you were because there was, at least, something good about it.

So when you're truly over the pain, you'll find yourself acknowledging the things that were good. You'll stop dissing the relationship all the time. And to be honest, you might even be caught smiling at some of the memories from that relationship, without it hurting.

And now, you're going to be taking some more responsibility. Because frankly, no one is perfect, not even you. So if we look deep, deep deep into all that happened, there's a chance you had even a tiny little role to play in how things turned out. Yes, it may have majorly been his fault, but there's very likely a part you played in the scheme, a part you have refused to admit to for a long time. But guess what, when you're finally over it, you will admit it and own your own stuff. Now, there's more clarity, and you're not ashamed to acknowledge that there's something you could have done better. And this is really one of the brightest signs of healing and of being in a good place for the new life you want to build, even for your relationship with other people.

And guess what! You finally stop stalking your ex. Admit it, you've been checking their Facebook and Instagram, looking out for what they've been up to, who's the new girl they're with, and all the stuff they've been doing. That's normal. Many people do that after a breakup because you just can't get over them, can't get used to the fact that they're no longer yours. But hasn't that also been such an exhausting experience? Keeping tabs on them on social media or maybe even using mutual friends to spy on them. It's exhausting, sis. It's a lot of work. And if you've been checking, stalking is notorious for a lot of emotional draining.

But when you've truly come into your healing, all that is history. You're living and letting them live. You're so busy building your new life that you really do not have the time or interest to do all that stalking anymore.

And sis, this place of absolute healing is where I can't wait for you to get to. I'm not going to pretend it is not a long walk, that it's not a tough road to travel. It is for everyone who's been there. It's a long, long walk but what matters is that you stay on track, and you get home eventually. One step at a time, you can do it.

You've come all the way, and you've come this far, you've fought many external and many internal battles, you've cried, and finally, you've healed. It's been a long walk, but slowly, surely, you made it home.

And I love to see you here. Don't give up this peace for anything. Stay on track. I'm rooting hard for you.

By the time you successfully work through your healing process and get back on the dating scene, you will approach dating differently. Instead of trying to be picked, you will carry yourself like the queen you are, and when someone tries to approach you...

Stare them right in the eye and say, "I understand why you want me, but why would I want you?"

Author Bio

Ever felt shredded by the weight of your divorce? There are times when a woman feels devastated by an unforeseen breakup or feels guilty leaving toxic relationships. These unguided times must take power from T. Marie The Break Coach. Tiffany Smith is the name that takes pride in helping women find their way to the glory of self-love.

Raised in New Jersey, Smith was a very keen writer. In her journey, she took pleasure in helping the community around her. Smith is an individual flag bearer to the idea of women empowerment. She always felt she had to plant her twigs in the garden, too. Smith went to a Historically Black College & University (HBCU) - Lincoln University in Pennsylvania state. In her college life, she harnessed her interest in writing and community service; she received a bachelors in Human Services. Syphoning a degree to her name, Smith stepped out in the world with her enriching aura looking for eyes that needed her help. The universe responded to her search when she went through a divorce. Smith experienced the tribulations of a breakup and found herself coiling back to unkempt decisions. Her qualms pinched open a whole new perspective for her; eventually, she became a Breakup Coach.

I UNDERSTAND WHY

It is truly fascinating how the universe knits your story. Likewise, Smith was dazzled by the idea of a Breakup Coach which she never anticipated. Smith advocates the concept of self-love as a top priority. Her transformation mantra presides over a five-prong rule: Acknowledge, Embrace, Acceptance, Forgiveness & Love Yourself. She owns a coaching platform named "Dare To B You, LLC". At "Dare To B You", Smith fashions women who have suffered breakups into independent self and assists them in rebuilding and repurposing their lives. Apart from 10 years of social services on the ground, she authors a book by the title: "I understand why you would want me but why would I want you?"

The book shares stories of women and builds on the ideas of growth, strength & self-love. Smith's dedication to helping women who are falling apart is truly tremendous and numerous women find warmth in her words and action.

www.ingramcontent.com/pod-product-compliance
Lightning Source LLC
Chambersburg PA
CBHW071433070526
44578CB00001B/94